The Socialist Alternative

THE SOCIALIST ALTERNATIVE
Real Human Development

by Michael A. Lebowitz

MONTHLY REVIEW PRESS

New York

Lebowitz, Michael A.
   The socialist alternative : real human development / by Michael Lebowitz.
      p. cm.
   Includes bibliographical references and index.
   ISBN 978-1-58367-215-0 — ISBN 978-1-58367-214-3 (pbk.)
   1. Socialism. I. Title.
   HX73.L4167 2010
   335—dc22

                              2010019380

Monthly Review Press
146 West 29th Street, Suite 6W
New York, New York 10001

www.monthlyreview.org
www.MRzine.org

5 4 3 2

Contents

For those who must struggle for a society in which wealth does not appear as an "immense collection of commodities" and where "the original sources of all wealth," human beings and nature, are not destroyed.

Preface

A specter is haunting the world—the specter of barbarism. Of course, that prospect has always been latent in capitalism because nothing matters for capital but profits; however, the drive for quantitative expansion that is inherent in capitalism has now generated an ecological crisis. And, as the limits of Earth become apparent, there inevitably arises the question of who is entitled to command increasingly limited resources. To whom will go the oil, the metals, the food, the water? The currently rich countries of capitalism, those that have been able to develop because others have not? The impoverished producers in the world? Following the capitalist path, we can be certain that force will decide—imperialism and barbarism.

The purpose of this book is to point to an alternative path. A path focused not upon quantitative growth but on the full development of human potential, not a path of barbarism but one of socialism. And the premise is that we desperately need a vision of that alternative. Because if we don't know where we want to go, no path will take us there.

To clarify and develop that vision, a number of concepts are explored in *The Socialist Alternative*: socialism as a process rather than a stage; human development as the core of socialism; the key link of human development and practice (which has as its implication the necessity for worker and community management); the understanding of the means of production as a social heritage that belongs properly to no subset of humanity; expansion of the commons in the construction of a solidarian society; socialist conditionality; socialist accountancy; and the socialist mode of regulation.

Where did these ideas come from? Well, certainly a major source is Marx. Indeed, much here extends my discussion of the "political economy of the working class" set out in *Beyond CAPITAL: Marx's Political Economy of the Working Class* (1992, 2003). Further, Marx's *Grundrisse* is especially important for insights into socialism itself—both because of its concept of an organic system and the distinction between the becoming and the being of such a system, and also because its discussion of self-interest versus communality is an essential link between Marx's earlier and later thoughts on this question.

Another source of ideas for this book comes from the years I spent teaching comparative economic systems. Some of my reflections on the experience of twentieth-century socialist efforts appear in a 1991 article, "The Socialist Fetter: A Cautionary Tale," where the concept of a socialist mode of regulation first surfaced (although not named as such until the following year). Indeed, the original conception of this book included a section on the "real socialism" of the USSR and Eastern Europe and one on the Yugoslav model; however, as I began to write about the question of real socialism, the section expanded from two chapters to five and was still growing! So, I decided to shift the analysis of these and other experiences to a separate project, *Studies in the Development of Socialism*. Nevertheless, readers will see clearly that the concept of socialism developed here is an alternative to both the real socialism of the Soviet model and the market self-management system of Yugoslavia.

I was surprised, though, to recognize how much here is the product of my personal experiences and activity. Certainly, there is the echo of my time in the Students for a Democratic Society with its slogan that decisions be made by those who are affected by them. Further, my activity in the New Democratic Party (NDP) of Canada (an education into the limits of social democracy) is reflected in strategies posed here for struggle within capitalism. Greatly influenced by the Institute for Workers Control in the United Kingdom, I developed policies for the British Columbia NDP (where I served as economic policy chair and policy chair in the early 1970s) for opening the books of corporations to government and workers and nationalizing firms unwilling to accept these new ground rules for a "good corporate citizen"—a definite precursor of the concept of "socialist conditionality" discussed in this book. Similarly, some themes here return to my work on free buses and neighborhood government for the 1972 NDP electoral efforts in Vancouver and my involvement in community organizing.

However, as will be seen, my experience in Venezuela has been most significant in shaping this volume. Not only the privilege of being present to learn from the exciting developments that have put socialism for the twenty-first century on the world agenda but also for the opportunity to participate in various ways, beginning in 2004, when I became advisor to the then-Ministry for the Social Economy. Some of my talks in Venezuela and reflections on the process there were included in *Build It Now: Socialism for the 21st Century*.

Although Venezuela is unique in many ways because of its rentist economy and culture, many of the problems that have emerged in the context of trying to build socialism are not. And we need to go beyond the particulars of that case to prepare ourselves for struggle everywhere. Accordingly, *The Socialist Alternative* draws upon the Venezuelan experiment to develop a *general* vision of socialism and concrete directions for struggle.

Although some specific ideas here (such as the elements of the "elementary triangle of socialism") emanate from position papers and my work with *Centro Internacional Miranda* in Caracas, this is not a book about the Bolivarian process in Venezuela. Yes, that process has definitely revealed the specter of socialism for the twenty-first century, but is that particular specter *real*? This question will be explored in *Studies in the Development of Socialism*.

Finally, this book would not have been written were it not for the encouragement and comradeship of Marta Harnecker. Her optimism, intelligence, and dedication to building socialism are a constant inspiration; and her work in Venezuela on participation, communal councils, and communes is an essential contribution to building socialism everywhere (as is her work on the political instrument in *Rebuilding the Left*).

Does it need to be stressed these days that socialism is not inevitable? As I noted in *Build It Now*, the title of that book came from the (I hope not forgotten) slogan of the South African Communist Party—"Socialism Is the Future, Build It Now!"—that stressed vision and struggle. The optimism of the intellect embodied in that slogan, though, needs to be corrected. Without a vision and the struggle to make that vision real, the future *is* inevitable—the alternative of barbarism. "Socialism *must be* the future, build it now."

—11 January 2010

Reinventing Socialism

What is a good society? What do we want—for ourselves, for our families, for those we love? What are the characteristics of a good society, one in which we would like to live, one to which we think everyone has a right?

For me, a good society is one that permits the full development of human potential. This is really the starting point—as it was for Marx and other nineteenth-century socialists. Saint-Simon viewed such a society as one that would provide to its members "the greatest possible opportunity for the development of their faculties." Similarly, for Louis Blanc, the goal was to ensure that everyone has "the *power* to develop and exercise his faculties in order to really be free." And Friedrich Engels indicated that the aim of the Communists was "to organize society in such a way that every member of it can develop and use all his capabilities and powers in complete freedom and without thereby infringing the basic conditions of this society."[1] Certainly, too, human development was central to Marx's perspective; he looked to a society where each individual is able to develop his full potential—that is, the "absolute working-out of his creative potentialities," the "complete working out of the human content," the "development of all human powers as such the end in itself."[2]

That this vision of a good society is alive today can clearly be seen in the Bolivarian Constitution of Venezuela. In its explicit recognition in Article 299 that the goal of a human society must be that of "ensuring overall human development," in the declaration of Article 20 that "everyone has the right to the free development of his or her own personality" and the focus of Article 102 upon "developing the creative potential of every human being and the full exercise of his or her personality in a democratic society"—the theme of human development pervades the Bolivarian Constitution.

But there is more. This Constitution also focuses upon the question of *how* people develop their capacities and capabilities— that is, *how* overall human development occurs. Article 62 declares that participation by people in "forming, carrying out and controlling the management of public affairs is the necessary way of achieving the involvement to ensure their complete development, both individual and collective." The *necessary* way. The same emphasis upon a democratic, participatory and protagonistic society is also present in the economic sphere, which is why Article 70 stresses "self-management, co-management, cooperatives in all forms" and why Article 102's goal of "developing the creative potential of every human being" emphasizes "active, conscious and joint participation."[3]

These themes in the Bolivarian Constitution of full human development and what human development requires both imply a particular theory. In the former case, it is a theory that stresses the gap between what is and what *ought* to be. Implicit is the recognition that the full development of our creative potential is not occurring but that it is *possible*. In other words, that what we observe now in the capacities of human beings is not *all* that is possible, that what we are now is a fraction of what we can be. It is a clear recognition that human development is not fixed and that we do not know its boundaries. This is, of course, a political statement—because it implies that there is an alternative.

Similarly, with respect to the second theme, the Constitution embodies a familiar theory in its insistence that participation is necessary for human development—Marx's concept of "revolutionary practice." The "coincidence of the changing of circumstances and of human activity or self-change" is the red thread that runs throughout Marx's work. Human development, he understood, does not drop from the sky; it is not the result of gifts from above. Rather, we change ourselves through our activity. As we will see, Marx's understanding of the simultaneous change in circumstances and self-change means that we are the products of all our activities—the products of our struggles (and our failure to struggle), the products of all the relations in which we produce and interact.

These two principles—the focus upon human development and upon practice and protagonism as the "necessary way"—constitute the *key link* we need to grasp. Once we do, we recognize that *without practice, you cannot have the full development of human capacities*. Without the protagonism that transforms people, you cannot produce the people who belong in the good society. This key link of human development and practice has profound implications, because it allows us to identify the paths that lead *not* to a good society but to a dead end.

A good society, though, is also one where people care about each other and understand that "the development of the human capacities on the one side [cannot be] based on the restriction of development on the other."4 It is based upon the concept of a human family where our relations (in the words of Article 75 of the Bolivarian Constitution) are based upon "equality of rights and duties, solidarity, common effort, mutual understanding and reciprocal respect." Rather than a collection of self-oriented individuals (and groups), the good society is one where we recognize "the obligations which, by virtue of solidarity, social responsibility and humanitarian assistance, are incumbent upon private individuals according to their abilities" (Article 135). Very simply, the good society, as the *Communist Manifesto* put it, is an association in which "the free development of each is the condition for the free development of all."

A PERVERSE SOCIETY

By the above criteria, no one could honestly say that capitalism is a good society. Capitalism is certainly not oriented toward solidarity, respect, social responsibility, or caring; it is not about creating the conditions for protagonism in workplaces and society— that necessary way by which people can achieve "their complete development, both individual and collective." On the contrary, capitalism is not about human development at all.

The logic of capital generates a society in which all human values are subordinated to the search for profits. How can the free development of workers occur when they are compelled to sell their ability to produce to capitalists for whom they are only a means to profit? Not only are workers exploited, but they are also deformed ("crippled," Marx said), both in the process of *producing* surplus value and by the constant generation of new needs in order to *realize* that surplus value. Rather than building a cohesive and caring society, capital tears society apart. It divides workers and pits them against one another as competitors to reduce any challenges to its rule and its bottom line. Precisely because human beings and nature are mere means to capital's goal, it destroys what Marx called the original sources of wealth—human beings and nature.

The perverse nature of capitalism shows itself most fully during periods of economic crises. Then it is possible to see that the rate of profit "determines the expansion or contraction of production, instead of the proportion between production and social needs, the needs of socially developed human beings." The inability of capitalists to make money causes them to bring production to a halt, irrespective of human needs.[5] The result is a combination of unemployed workers, underutilized capacities and resources, and people with unmet needs. Production could occur, but it does not. Why? Simply because it is not profitable for those who own the means of production. What more evidence of the irrationality of capitalism is needed? In fact, the system is so profoundly perverse that it is necessary to ask, *What keeps capitalism going?*

CAPITALISM AS AN ORGANIC SYSTEM

What allows this system to renew itself? What are its structural requirements, its conditions of existence? To understand the reproduction of capitalism, we have to think of it as a total, connected process—as a "structure of society, in which all relations coexist simultaneously and support one another." In capitalism, Marx explained, "every economic relation presupposes every other in its bourgeois economic form, and everything posited is thus also a presupposition; this is the case with every organic system."[6]

The starting point for grasping capitalism as an organic system is to see it as a relationship between capitalists, who are the owners of the means of production and driven by the desire for profits (surplus value), and workers, who are separated from means of production and thus have no alternative to maintain themselves but to sell their capacity to perform labor (labor power). This is the logical premise of capitalism, and this presupposition (capitalists who own the means of production and workers who must sell their labor power) also must be demonstrated to be the result.

Capital's purchase of labor power immediately gives it the right to supervise and direct workers in the labor process and gives it the property rights to what the workers produce. It uses these rights to exploit workers, that is, to compel the performance of surplus labor. Production of commodities that contain surplus value thus occurs in the sphere of production under capitalist productive relations. What capital wants, though, is not those impregnated commodities but to make that surplus value real, in the form of money, by selling those commodities.

With the successful sale of those commodities (and thus the realization of the surplus value), capital is able to renew the means of production consumed in the process of production, hire wage laborers again, maintain its own desired consumption, and accumulate capital for the purpose of expansion. Thus capital is reproduced and grows. Its ability to continue to operate as capital, however, requires the reproduction of workers as wage laborers (workers who must reappear in the labor market to sell their labor power in order to survive); this latter condition is "the absolutely necessary condition for capitalist production."[7] And that necessity to sell labor power once again is reproduced when the wages that workers obtain are spent upon their customary requirements, which are then consumed. So, back to the labor market.

The production, distribution, and consumption characteristic of capitalism all support one another to ensure its reproduction as an organic system. Production under capitalist relations reproduces capitalist distribution relations; capitalism, in short, is a system not only of production but also one of reproduction:

> The capitalist process of production, therefore, seen as a total, connected process, i.e. a process of reproduction, produces not only commodities, not only surplus value, but also produces and reproduces the capital-relation itself; on one hand the capitalist, on the other the wage labourer.[8]

Of course, it's not quite that automatic. If the reproduction of capital requires the reproduction of workers as wage laborers (in other words, that they continue to sell their labor power), what *ensures* this? While capital constantly tries to drive wages down, workers push in the opposite direction. So what ensures that workers will not gain sufficient wages to extract themselves from the need to sell their ability to work in order to survive?

One way capital keeps wages down is by dividing and separating workers so they compete against one another rather than combine against capital. Not only does capital do this by using workers against one another (as Marx described the manner in which capital took advantage of the hostility between English and Irish workers) but it also does this by constantly reproducing a reserve army of the unemployed through the substitution of machinery for workers. The competition among workers and the division of the working class into employed and unemployed both tend to keep wages down. That is, as Marx commented, "the great beauty of capitalist production":

> It not only constantly reproduces the wage labourer as a wage labourer, but also always produces a relative surplus population of wage labourers in proportion to the accumulation of capital.

The result is that wages are "confined within limits satisfactory to capitalist exploitation, and lastly, the social dependence of the worker on the capitalist, which is indispensable, is secured."[9] Add to this the fact that workers' needs to consume grow as the result of the combination of the alienation (the impoverishment, the "complete emptying-out") characteristic of capitalist production and the constant generation of new needs by capital in its attempt to sell commodities, and it is easy to see why workers are compelled to continually present themselves in the labor market.[10]

What we can observe clearly here is *the vicious circle of capitalism*. Beginning with (a) people who are separated from the means of production and with needs they must fulfill, we see that these people (b) must go into the labor market to sell their labor power—competing with other people in the same situation. They (c) enter into capitalist production, that process which yields as its result impoverished workers with both the need and the means to consume. Having (d) consumed the products they are able to purchase, however, they are once again without the means to maintain themselves and must present themselves again to capital; they must once again produce for capital's goals. This is a vicious circle, and its phases are interdependent—you cannot change one without changing them all.

As we will see in the first chapter, though, it is not only capital's ability to displace workers that ensures the "indispensable" social dependence of the worker on the capitalist. Capital continues to rule over production and society, Marx argued, because workers think capital is *necessary*. Indeed, capital tends to produce the working class it *needs*:

> The advance of capitalist production develops a working class which by education, tradition and habit looks upon the requirement of that mode of production as self-evident natural laws. The organization of the capitalist process of production, once it is fully developed, breaks down all resistance.[11]

In short, "in the completed bourgeois system, every economic relation presupposes every other in its bourgeois economic form."

As long as workers do not understand that capital is the result of exploitation, they will always be dependent upon it—no matter how much they may struggle on particular questions, such as questions of "fairness" (e.g., "fair" wages). And that is why Marx wrote *Capital*. Precisely because of capital's inherent tendency to develop a working class that looks upon capital's requirements as "self-evident natural laws," Marx's purpose was to explain the

nature of capital to workers and to help them una
necessity to go beyond capitalism.[12]

Understanding that capitalism is a perverse socie
deforms people and that capital, itself, is the result of explo.
is not enough, however. If people think there is no alterna. ,e,
then they will struggle to do their best within capitalism but will
not waste their time and energy trying to achieve the impossible.
For that very reason, a vision of an alternative is essential.

THE SPECTER OF SOCIALISM
FOR THE TWENTY-FIRST CENTURY

Marx had a vision of an alternative—the society of associated producers, "a society of free individuality, based on the universal
development of individuals and on their subordination of their
communal, social productivity as their social wealth."[13] Socialism
for him was a society that removes all obstacles to the full development of human beings; it was one in which "the worker's own
need for development" guides society. The possibility of that
"good society" was indeed the perspective from which he criticized capitalism; it is the *premise* of his book, *Capital*.[15]

Rather than this focus upon the full development of human
potential, however, the dominant conception of socialism in the
twentieth century tended to stress the development of productive
forces, a development that someday (and somehow) would produce a society that negated the unsatisfied needs characteristic of
capitalism—a society characterized by an abundance that would
allow everyone to consume and consume in accordance with their
needs. An important part of the socialist vision was lost—human
beings at the center.

Unfortunately, too, a significant part of the image conveyed by
"socialism" and "communism" was that of a state standing over
and above society, one that directs and oppresses working peo-

ple—a bitter irony, given Marx's contempt for the "all-directing bureaucracy" and the "state parasites, richly paid sycophants and sinecurists" of the state of mid-nineteenth-century France, a state that squeezed "the living civil society like a boa constrictor."[15]

"We have to reinvent socialism"—here was the statement with which Hugo Chávez electrified activists in his closing speech at the January 2005 World Social Forum in Porto Alegre, Brazil. "It can't be the kind of socialism that we saw in the Soviet Union," he stressed, "but it will emerge as we develop new systems that are built on cooperation, not competition." If we are ever going to end the poverty of the majority of the world, capitalism must be transcended, Chávez argued. "But we cannot resort to state capitalism, which would be the same perversion of the Soviet Union. We must reclaim socialism as a thesis, a project and a path, but a new type of socialism, a humanist one, which puts humans and not machines or the state ahead of everything."[16]

In short, neither expansion of the means of production nor direction by the state should define the new socialist society; rather, human beings must be at its center. *This is the specter that is haunting capitalism—the specter of socialism for the twenty-first century*. At its core is the "key link" of human development and practice—the premise that the development of human capacities can occur only through practice and that thus points to our need to be able to develop through democratic, participatory, and protagonistic activity in every aspect of our lives. Through revolutionary practice in our communities, our workplaces, and in all our social institutions, we produce ourselves as other than the impoverished and crippled human beings that capitalism produces.

The process by which the outlines of this specter emerged in Venezuela is clear. As we have seen, the Bolivarian Constitution of 1999 contained definite elements that pointed in the direction of the good society. At the same time, though, that constitution clearly supported the maintenance of capitalism—a "good capitalism," the Third Way which Chávez at that point desired.[17] His belief in the possibility of a capitalist road, however, essentially ended with the thwarted coup of 2002 and the capitalist lockout of oil and other sectors in the winter of 2002–3—demonstrations that Venezuelan capitalists and their imperialist supporters were not *interested* in a "good capitalism."

In the wake of these developments, the Bolivarian process shifted significantly to the left. There was still no open talk of socialism. Rather, the "social economy" was offered as the alternative to capitalism. Thus, on his *Alo Presidente* program of September 14, 2003, Chávez announced that "the logic of capital is a perverse logic." Capital, he argued, doesn't care about putting children to work, about the hunger of workers, about the malnutrition of their children. It is not interested in labor accidents, if workers eat, if they have housing, where they sleep, if they have schools, if when they get sick they have doctors, if when they are old they have a pension. "No. The logic of capital cares nothing about that, it is diabolical, it is perverse."

In contrast, Chávez argued that "the social economy bases its logic on the human being, on work, that is to say, on the worker and the worker's family, that is to say, in the human being." This social economy also does not focus on economic gain, on exchange values; rather "the social economy generates mainly use-value." Its purpose is "the construction of the new man, of the new woman, of the new society."[18] In fact, by 2003, Chávez was talking about socialism without the use of the term.

Chávez's announcement in early 2005 of the need to "reinvent socialism" was just the beginning, and his ideas about socialism increasingly took shape in 2005 as he immersed himself in *Beyond Capital*, "the wonderful book of István Mészáros." From this thousand-page book, Chávez's orientation toward use-values rather than exchange values was reinforced by Mészáros's reading of Marx's *Grundrisse* critique of commodity exchange in the new society.[19] Excited by Marx's argument that the communal economy requires an exchange not of things but of *activities*—activities determined by communal needs and communal purposes, Chávez called in July for creation of "a communal system of production and consumption, a new system."[20] This would be the way to build solidarity, cooperation, complementarity, reciprocity, justice, equality, and sustainability—all those characteristics contrary to the logic of capital (*Alo Presidente* # 229).

Following his reelection in December 2006, Chávez's presentation of the socialist alternative deepened. In January 2007, he introduced the concept of "the elementary triangle of socialism"—the combination of social property, social production, and satisfaction of social needs (*Alo Presidente* #264 but see also #263). Consider the logic underlying this particular combination: (a) social ownership of the means of production is critical because it is the only way to ensure that our communal, social productivity is directed to the free development of all; (b) social production organized by workers builds new relations of cooperation among producers and is a condition for the full development of the producers; and (c) production for communal needs and purposes is inherent in a solidarian society, one which recognizes that the free development of each is the condition for the free development of all. All of these were connected, interdependent—three sides of "the elementary socialist triangle."[21]

Once again, Chávez's theoretical step can be traced back to Mészáros's *Beyond Capital*. Drawing upon Marx, Mészáros had argued the necessity to understand capitalism as an organic system, a specific combination of production-distribution-consumption, in which all the elements coexist simultaneously and support one another. The failure of the socialist experiments of the twentieth century, he proposed, occurred because of the failure to go beyond "the vicious circle of the capital relation," the combination of circuits "all intertwined and mutually reinforcing one another" that thereby reinforced "the perverse dialectic of the incurably wasteful capital system." In short, the lack of success (or

effort) in superseding all parts of "the totality of existing repro-
ductive relations" meant the failure to go "beyond capital."[22]

Thus, Mészáros stressed the need to restructure all of the
parts of capitalism's organic system. The socialist alternative
requires "the radical reconstitution of the dialectic of production-
distribution-consumption, setting out from the genuine social
control of the means of production."[23] Here, then, was the underlying concept that led ultimately to "the elementary triangle of
socialism": social property, social production, social needs.

The promising path that the concept of the socialist triangle
opens up is the theme of this book. *The Socialist Alternative: Real
Human Development* is divided into two sections. The opening
part, "The Socialist Triangle,'" contains chapters on "the wealth
of people," "the production of people," and "the solidarian society." Part II, "Building the Socialist Triangle," includes several
chapters on the concept of socialist transition and on concrete
measures for building the good society. There is a reason for this
division and sequence.

While the specter of socialism for the twenty-first century has
appeared (with much more material substance than the specter
Marx and Engels described in the mid-nineteenth century) and
has grasped the minds of masses in Venezuela and elsewhere, it
has not been realized yet. Socialism for this century needs to be
built—a task of special importance given that *other* specter that is
haunting us, the specter of barbarism. And, as I argued in
"Socialism Does Not Drop from the Sky," we need to understand
that the process of building it will differ everywhere:

> Every society has its unique characteristics—its unique histo-
> ries, traditions (including religious and indigenous ones), its
> mythologies, its heroes who have struggled for a better world
> and the particular capacities that people have developed in the
> process of struggle. Since we are talking about a process of
> human development and not abstract recipes, we understand

that we proceed most surely when we choose our own path, one which people recognize as their own (rather than the pale imitation of someone else).

Add to that different levels of economic development, differing correlations of political forces (nationally and internationally), and the different historical actors who start us on the path, and it is clear that "we would be pedantic fools if we insisted that there is only one way to start the social revolution."[24]

But we *do* need to know where we want to go. There's an old saying that if you don't know where you want to go, then any road will take you there. The saying is wrong, though. If you don't know where you want to go, then *no* road will take you there.

PART 1

The Socialist Triangle

1. The Wealth of People

Return to the concept of the good society—one with human beings at the center. We described the good society as one that fosters the full development of human potential, ensures the protagonism that is the necessary condition for complete development, and encourages solidarity and caring. The good society is a wealthy society. But what is the basis of a wealthy society?

According to Adam Smith, the key determinant of wealth, defined as the use-values that a society produces, is the productive power of labor; that is, the higher the level of society's productivity, the greater the quantity of use-values produced for a given population. The starting point, of course, is human beings and nature—what Marx called "the original sources of wealth." Whereas nature provides the original basis for life, human beings transform the raw materials that come from nature into use-values that are the substance of wealth.

Besides human beings and nature, another factor is critical in determining the quantity of use-values that can be produced in a given period—the instruments of labor with which human beings transform raw materials. When an individual devotes time to create a tool (for example, a Robinson Crusoe making a trap or a net or a simple plow), he increases the quantity of use-values he will be able to obtain subsequently. In short, his productivity increases as the result of the dedication of some of his labor to the production of instruments of labor.

Clearly, the results of past labor are an important factor in producing wealth measured as use-values. How important they are, though, will depend on how long they last. Thus instruments of labor that last only one season or one year will obviously have to be replaced quickly (and thus require the allocation of labor to this end); in contrast, durable instruments that do not require replacement for long periods of time can continue to contribute to productivity.

Further, labor-time that is not needed to replace instruments of labor that are consumed can be used to accumulate more instruments of labor—more nets, more traps, and so forth. Insofar as durable instruments continue in use without the need to devote labor for their replacement, they perform "the same free service as the forces of nature, such as water, steam, air, and electricity. This free service of past labour, when it is seized on and filled with vitality by living labour, accumulates progressively as accumulation takes place on a larger and larger scale."[1] More and more, then, the productivity of labor can be the result of the "free service of past labour."

Of course, we are describing the development of *social* productivity. The productive power of individual, isolated people is very low. Indeed, the concept of isolated individuals is a myth because we live in society (even if this is only a family). There is a reason, though, for people to cooperate. Marx noted that cooperation results in "the creation of a new productive power, which is intrinsically a collective one."[2] For example, the combination of individuals for building a road is more than just an addition of their individual labor capacities: "The unification of their forces," he observed, "increases their *force of production*."[3]

So, in all societies people find ways to cooperate—whether it is by specializing or by working together by combining similar labor—precisely because our social productivity is increased by the combination of labor; that is, because of the benefits available from *"united, combined labour."* [4] Adam Smith certainly understood the importance of the combination of labor—both within the individual workplace (for example, the pin factory) and within the society—for the increase in social productivity. His emphasis, however, was upon the *division* of labor, which was the consequence of a "certain propensity in human nature . . . the propensity to truck, barter, and exchange one thing for another" (which, of course, had nothing to do with the pin factory). In contrast, we stress not the division of labor (which is but one form of cooperation and presupposes cooperation) but the *combination* of labor—its character as social labor.[5]

Thus in the "association of the workers—the cooperation and division of labour as fundamental conditions of the productivity of labour," we see what Marx and Engels called in *The German Ideology* "the multiplied productive force, which arises through the co-operation of different individuals as it is caused by the division of labour."[6] This is a central proposition of the political economy of the working class that I identified in *Beyond CAPITAL*: "any co-operation and combination of labour in production generates a combined, social productivity of labour that exceeds the sum of individual, isolated productivities."[7] Very simply, as Marx noted, "the social productive power which arises from co-operation is a *free gift.*"[8]

When we work with the results of past labor, this too is the product of the combination of labor. Those tools, machines, improvements to land, and intellectual and scientific discoveries that substantially increase social productivity are available for use by living labor because of the previous allocation of labor to those activities. Both within specific workplaces and within society as a whole, some producers create means of production that increase the productivity of others; total social productivity increases—the more so, the more advanced and long-lasting the particular means of production in question. The heritage of past labor, our social inheritance, is there for generation after generation.

And we inherit and use more than tools, machines, the *things* that are the products of human society. "The accumulation of knowledge and of skill, of the general productive forces of the social brain" becomes a growing source of productive power over time. Incorporated in the process of producing use-values, science becomes a productive force. The organs of human industry (the limbs of the physical productive apparatus) are *"organs of the human brain, created by the human hand*; the power of knowledge, objectified." Indeed, the growth of social productivity increasingly depends upon the extent that science, intellectual labor, "the general productive forces of the social brain" are incorporated into the production process:

> This development in productivity can always be reduced in the last analysis to the social character of the labour that is set to work, to the division of labour within society, and to the development of intellectual labour, in particular of the natural sciences.[9]

In this respect, Marx was very clear that our ability to produce wealth as use-values for people depends more and more *not* upon immediate and direct labor but upon the results of past social labor—the means of production that incorporate "general social knowledge [which] has become a *direct force of production*." Clearly, "to the degree that large industry develops, the creation of real wealth comes to depend less on labour time and on the amount of labour employed than on the power of the agencies set in motion during labour time." Indeed, direct labor itself becomes an "indispensable but subordinate moment, compared to general scientific labour, technological application of natural sciences, on the one side, and the general productive forces arising from social combination in total production on the other side—a combination which appears as a natural fruit of social labour (although it is a historical product)."10

Wealth as use-values is thus the result of this social combination—the result of people working with nature and the products of past labor, people creating products that maintain and enhance the original sources of wealth and provide the basis for increasing the future productive power of labor. We don't produce nature, but our social inheritance is our product and the product of past generations of workers. *But to whom does our social heritage belong?*

Not to us. "One of the chief factors in historical development up till now," Marx and Engels proposed in *The German Ideology*, is the "consolidation of what we ourselves produce into a material power above us." Here indeed is what they called the muck of ages: "man's own deed becomes an alien power opposed to him, which enslaves him instead of being controlled by him." All the wealth produced by workers ("the social power, i.e., the multiplied productive force, which arises through the co-operation of different individuals") appears as "not their own united power, but as an alien force existing outside them."11

THE MYSTIFICATION OF CAPITAL

There is a reason for this. Our power does not appear as our power because, in reality, it *isn't* our power anymore. Rather, we think of the means of production, of our social heritage, as *capital*. And what is capital? What is this money for which we sell our labor power, these objects of labor upon which we work, these tools, machines, instruments that we use in production? What are these products that sit in stores and that we work to obtain?

This was the central point Marx attempted to explain—the essence of that power above us, the essence of capital. His answer was unequivocal: it is the workers' own product that has been turned against them, a product in the form of tools, machinery—indeed, all the products of human activity (mental and manual). What you see when you look at capital is the result of past exploitation.

Insofar as workers sell their capacity to work to the owner of the means of production in order to satisfy their needs, they surrender all property rights in the products they produce. By purchasing the right to dispose of the worker's power, the capitalist has purchased the right to exploit the worker in production; and the result of that exploitation goes into the accumulation of more means of production. The power over us represented by the means of production, in short, is the power yielded to capital by generations of wage laborers.

Precisely because workers have sold their power to the capitalist, the "association of the workers—the cooperation and division of labour as fundamental conditions of the productivity of labour—appears as the *productive power of capital*. The collective power of labour, its character as social labour, is therefore the *collective power* of capital"; and the "free gift" that arises from the combination of labor is *a gift to capital*.[12] Further, all the fruits of past social labor accrue to the capitalist. Fixed capital, machinery, technology, science—all are only present wearing their "antagonistic social mask" as capital.[13] In short, "the accumulation of knowledge and of skill, of the general productive forces of the social brain, is thus absorbed into capital, as opposed to labour, and hence appears as an attribute of capital."[14]

But why doesn't everyone recognize that this social heritage is our own product turned against us? Why doesn't everyone understand that capital is the result of exploitation? The key, Marx emphasized, is that the exploitation of workers is not *obvious*. It doesn't *look* like the worker sells her ability to work and that the capitalist then proceeds to extract as much labor from that labor power as possible. Rather, it looks like the worker sells a certain amount of her *time* (a day's labor) to the capitalist and that she gets its *equivalent* in money.

What is the significance of the distinction that Marx made between labor power (the worker's capacity) and labor (the worker's activity)? When we focus upon the sale of labor power, we are thinking about the reproduction of the worker and thus her ability to work—that is, the necessary reproduction of the worker's availability to capital. This is the point made in the preceding chapter: "the absolutely necessary condition for capitalist production" is "the reproduction of workers as wage laborers" (as workers who must reappear in the labor market in order to survive). For Marx, here was one of the great contributions of classical political economy—the recognition that the wage was related to the reproduction of the worker. It was a point developed by the Physiocrats and followed by Adam Smith, "like all economists worth speaking of."[15]

But if we think that what workers sell is a particular quantity of labor, what ensures the reproduction of workers? How does capitalism continue? This, after all, was a central question for Marx. But that is not a question that any individual capitalist or worker is thinking about. It is the last thing on their minds. What an individual capitalist wants is not the reproduction of capitalism but his own reproduction, and for this he needs a particular quantity of labor. Thus, on the surface, it necessarily seems that the worker sells a particular quantity of her labor and gets its value. Indeed, that appearance is reinforced by the very form in which wages are stated (a wage for a given number of hours of work)—"all labour appears as paid labour."[16]

It is impossible to exaggerate the significance that Marx attached to this wage-form, which "extinguishes every trace of the division of the working day into necessary and surplus labour, into paid labour and unpaid labour." For Marx, the wage-form (which makes it appear that labor is purchased and fully paid for) is the basis for the mystification of capital:

All the notions of justice held by both the worker and the capitalist, all the mystifications of the capitalist mode of production, all capitalism's illusions about freedom, all the apologetic tricks of vulgar economics, have as their basis the form of appearance discussed above, which makes the actual relation invisible, and indeed presents to the eye the precise opposite of that relation.[17]

In that *"actual relation,"* the worker has sold the property right to command her labor power (which in itself yields an indeterminate quantity of labor) and has thereby yielded to the capitalist the right to extract as much labor as he can and the rights to all the fruits of exploitation. But if it seems (as it *must* seem on the surface) that the worker receives in exchange the equivalent of her labor, if it seems that there is no exploitation, then where do profits come from? *It must be from the contribution of the capitalist.* Just like the worker, he must get what he deserves.

And thus, if the capitalist is making a contribution to production at a given point, he must be *necessary*. Productivity gains also seem to be the result of what the capitalist does rather than the result of the combination of social labor. As we have seen, the development of new productive forces occurs through the allocation of a portion of society's labor to the production of new instruments of labor (including science, social intelligence, and the like). But what is the social agency in a capitalist economy by which society can make a decision to allocate labor for this purpose?

Just as in other societies characterized by exploitation, those who have exploited can use the surpluses resulting from that exploitation as they choose. Given the orientation of capital to the greatest possible growth, the capitalist uses a portion of his surplus value for the purpose of accumulation. The premise of this process remains exploitation, but the mystifying *form* through which this allocation of society's labor occurs is by capitalists allocating a sum of the *representative of social labor* they own—"money"; that is, by investing surplus value in its money-form.

THE WEALTH OF PEOPLE

The result is that the productivity gains arising from the accumulation of the "general productive forces of the social brain" necessarily appear to be the result of capitalist investment. Indeed, *all*
progress seems to depend upon "the accumulation of capital."

Of course, given capital's impulse to grow, capitalist progress
is of a particular type. The prerequisite of the growth of capital is
the growth of surplus value. Thus capital searches not for *any*
development of the productive forces but rather for developments
that will enhance its ability to expand the production and realization of surplus value. In short, the progress that capital seeks is a
biased progress; it is one which requires that capital (rather than
workers) can capture the fruits of productivity gain.[18] Science and
the technological application of science are there to serve capital:

> It becomes the task of science to be a means for the production of
> wealth; a means of enrichment. . . . *Exploitation of science*, of the
> theoretical progress of humanity. Capital does not create science,
> but it exploits it, appropriates it to the production process.[19]

Precisely because exploitation is hidden, all this is obscured.
Rather than going behind the "social mask" of capital to understand that it is the combination of living social labor and of past
social labor which is the source of growing productivity, we attribute all progress to capital. And the more the system develops, the
more that production relies upon fixed capital, the "organs of the
human brain, created by the human hand," the social heritage that
takes the form of instruments of labor—the more that capital (and
the capitalist) appear to be necessary to workers. Thus capitalism
tends to produce the workers it needs, workers who treat capitalism as common sense:

> The advance of capitalist production develops a working class
> which by education, tradition and habit looks upon the require-
> ments of this mode of production as self-evident natural laws.

The organization of the capitalist process of production, once it
is fully developed, breaks down all resistance.[20]

Indeed, all the dominant ideas in capitalism, all that appears to
be rational, are the ideas and rationality of the dominant class in
capitalism.[21] And this continues as long as capital owns the products of past social labor. As long as our social heritage, the product of generations of workers, belongs to capital, workers remain
under the control of capital. They remain (like nature) mere
means for capital's thrust to expand. As a result, capital tends to
destroy those original sources of wealth. Driving down wages to
their minimum, extending the length and intensity of the workday
to the maximum—all make sense for capital in its drive for profits.
And so too the constant generation of new needs for workers in
order for capital to be able to sell its commodities. As long as capital owns the means of production, our social inheritance, it is the
basis for the maintenance of exploitation, deformation, and the
destruction of the environment.

DISTRIBUTION: THE SOCIAL OWNERSHIP
OF THE MEANS OF PRODUCTION

We are now at the point where we need to consider the first side
of the "elementary triangle of socialism." Social ownership of the
results of social labor, social ownership of our social heritage, is
the only way to ensure that these are used in the interests of society and not for private gain. Rather than capitalist ownership of
the means of production, a socialist society requires a different
pattern of distribution of productive elements—social property,
social ownership of the means of production.

But what is social ownership of the means of production? It is
not the same as state ownership—something that the twentieth
century clearly demonstrated. If state bureaucrats and party func-

tionaries determine the goals of production and direct the use of means of production and discipline workers to achieve those goals, how could we think of this as social ownership, as ownership by society?

The experience of the twentieth century, accordingly, produced an alternative conception, one articulated well by Pat Devine in his classic 1988 book *Democracy and Economic Planning*.[22] In that conception, social ownership can be said to exist where all those affected by decisions about the use of means of production are involved in *deciding* upon that use. Thus workers in those productive units (as well as those who work in supplying units and in the units using that output) in addition to members of affected communities need to be involved in directing the use of means of production. In other words, social ownership by this definition necessarily implies a profound democracy from below rather than decisions by a state that stands over and above society.

And yet we need to ask whether this definition, though necessary, is *sufficient*. Even if means of production are socially owned in this sense, those means of production are discrete and separate. Particular means of production are possessed within *different* productive units, and not everyone has equal access to those means of production owned in common.[23] In other words, there is differential access to the means of production. This can be significant. One need only recall the experience of workers in collective enterprises in China compared to those in state-owned enterprises, of workers in the textile industry in Yugoslavia compared to those in the electric power sector, and of workers in the tourist sector in Cuba compared to those in sugar refineries to understand—*the means of production may belong to everyone but it may matter where you work!*

If some producers are able to secure particular benefits (for example, higher incomes) as the result of privileged access to particular means of production, their advantage is the product of monopoly—the ability to exclude others from particular means of production.[24] How, then, could this qualify as *social* ownership of the means of production? Clearly, a definition of social ownership of the means of production limited to the form of decision-making over the use of specific means of production may validate current and historic inequalities among people. Is that compatible with socialism as an organic system?

Consideration of distribution within socialism as an organic system and of social ownership of the means of production leads, therefore, to the question, "*Who is entitled?*" Who is entitled to the fruits of past and present social labor? Who is entitled to enjoy our social heritage? This central question brings us directly to Marx's concept of the wealth of people—to Marx's concept of *real* wealth.

RICH HUMAN BEINGS

In capitalism, as we've seen, all is subordinated to capital's goal—accumulate, accumulate wealth as capital. But the alternative in a rational society is not to accumulate, accumulate *things*. It is perfectly understandable why people within a capitalist society desire and view as necessities the commodities that capital has been trying to sell them. Capitalistically generated needs constantly grow; indeed, Marx commented that "the contemporary power of capital" rests upon the creation of new needs for workers.[25] Nevertheless, things are not real wealth. Having greater quantities of things—"Who has the most toys?"—does not make people really wealthy.

In short, we need to go beyond a conception of wealth that merely substitutes for a quantity of money a quantity of things—an example of how capital has deformed our conceptions. Marx had such an alternative conception. Right from the outset, Marx rejected the preoccupations of the political economists of his time and envisioned a "rich human being"—one who has developed his capacities and capabilities to the point where he is able "to take gratification in a many-sided way"—"the *rich* man *profoundly endowed with all the senses.*" "In place of the *wealth* and *poverty* of political economy," Marx proposed, "come the *rich human being* and rich *human* need. The *rich* human being is simultaneously the human being *in need of* a totality of human manifestations of life—the man in whom his own realisation exists as an inner necessity, as *need.*"[26]

It was not only the young Marx, however, who spoke so eloquently about rich human beings. In the *Grundrisse*, Marx *continued* to stress the centrality of the concept of rich human beings. "When the limited bourgeois form is stripped away," he asked, "what is wealth other than the universality of individual needs, capacities, pleasures, productive forces etc., created through universal exchange?"[27] In continuing to envision a rich human being—"as rich as possible in needs, because rich in qualities and relations . . . as the most total and universal possible social product," Marx revealed his understanding that *real wealth is the development of human capacity.*[28]

Grasping this concept is essential if we are to understand the perspective from which Marx proceeded: real wealth is the development of human capacities, the development of human potential. Marx's concept encompassed the capabilities of both production and consumption because the development of the ability to enjoy is "the development of an individual potential."[29] In short, there was no contradiction between saying, on the one hand, that "real wealth is the developed productive power of all individuals" and, on the other, that "regarded *materially*, wealth consists only in the manifold variety of needs."[30] Rather than thinking of a being with simple needs and simple productive powers, Marx looked to the "development of the rich individuality which is as all-sided in its production as in its consumption."[31]

This is what Marx's conception of socialism was all about— the creation of a society that removes all obstacles to the full development of human beings. In contrast to a society where the worker exists to satisfy the need of capital for its growth, he looked to what he called in *Capital* "the inverse situation, in which objective wealth is there to satisfy the worker's own need for development."[32]

In that society of associated producers, each individual is able to develop his full potential—that is, the "absolute working-out of his creative potentialities," the "complete working-out of the human content," the "development of all human powers as such the end in itself."[33] In socialism, the productive forces would have "increased with the all-around development of the individual, and all the springs of co-operative wealth flow more abundantly."[34] The result, in short, would be the production of rich human beings.

This is the real wealth of people—rich human beings. Quality rather than quantity. Obviously *capitalism* does not produce rich human beings—indeed, just the opposite! Because that is not capital's goal. In capitalism, human beings are not the end; rather, they are means for the expansion of capital. In capitalism, we are dominated by our own products—there is the "consolidation of what we ourselves produce into a material power above us." The "objective wealth" we create is not there to satisfy the worker's own need for development; rather, we exist in a society that inverts the relation between the products of labor and human development.

Clearly, it is essential to end capital's right to our social heritage—that is, to make capitalist property the property of society. But is that enough? Capital dominates within capitalism not simply because we have created a power that now controls us—a Frankenstein monster that enslaves us. Yes, our products are a power over us—but not simply because they are a power. It is also because *we are not*. Capitalism does not simply impoverish us because it extracts from us the things we produce. It impoverishes us because of the people it produces.

How, then, are *rich* human beings produced? How do we ensure that everyone has the opportunity for the full development of her potential? We now move to the second element within the socialist combination, where we will consider this question.

2. The Production of People

Think about Marx's concept of rich human beings. There is much current talk about human development as, for example, in the Human Development Reports published by the United Nations Development Program. But there is a difference in these conceptions, and that difference centers around the "key link" of human development and practice.

The Human Development Reports, which dramatically move away from the crude identification of development with statistics on economic growth, draw in particular upon the theoretical work of the economist Amartya Sen. In this work, the central focus is upon the development of human capabilities, which is sometimes described as the "capabilities approach." The development of human capabilities is seen as at the core of human development and as the condition for people to be able to live lives of respect and value.[1]

But what people influenced by this approach focus upon is the removal of barriers. Having capabilities for them is having opportunities. So this approach stresses the broadening of opportunities—for example, removing racism, removing sexism, removing inadequate education, removing conditions that gener-

ate poor health, removing restrictions on the opportunities for
people to have a life of dignity.

In this context Human Development Reports record the
achievements of different societies in terms of what is provided in
areas such as education and health. This is important and very
revealing, but the reports are not an attempt to measure human
capability as such; rather, they basically tell us about the effect of
some government priorities for expenditures. Accordingly, they
say nothing about how the *struggle* to end racism, sexism, and
inequality in education and health transforms people. Or how
engaging in cooperative production or learning in the workplace
how to manage production develops the capacities of people. In
short, the reports say nothing about the role of human activity.
Rather, their focus is upon creating a level playing field and
removing the barriers to equality that restrict opportunities.

Essentially, this perspective is liberal reformist. It certainly
rejects the neoliberal worship of the market with all its inhuman
effects, and it accepts the importance of the role of the state in
supporting human welfare. However, it implicitly argues that
broadening and equalizing opportunities—something that states
should do—is the answer to neoliberalism. The difference
between this perspective and the key link is most obvious when it
comes to talking about education.

In the Human Development Reports, what matters is how
much states choose to spend on education—that is, what their priorities are. What proportion of the society is illiterate? What proportion has completed high school? What proportion has gone to
university? And, this approach logically asks, too, about gender differences in this data—in order to explore the effect of sexism and
patriarchy in preventing human development. Do all castes and
races have the opportunity for education or are they excluded?

But what it doesn't ask is—what *kind* of education? Is it education delivered vertically from the top to the bottom? Is it education that involves the memorization by students of accepted

truths? Truths accepted by and acceptable to those at the top? Is it education that supports the maintenance of existing power structures? Or is it education as a process in which people learn through their own activity?

These are the very types of questions posed by Paulo Freire, who was himself profoundly influenced by Marx. Freire distinguished very clearly between the delivery of "banked knowledge" and knowledge that develops from a critical process that examines the world and our place in the world. "In the banking concept of knowledge," Freire pointed out, "knowledge is a gift bestowed by those who consider themselves knowledgeable upon those whom they consider to know nothing."[2] In other words, it is a gift from above. The state provides a gift; the teacher provides a gift.

In contrast, Freire's own concept of education—what he calls "problem-posing education"—stressed revolutionary practice: the relation between our activity and the development of our capacities. "Problem-posing education," he noted, "affirms men and women as being in the process of *becoming*—as unfinished, uncompleted beings"; it is a "humanist and liberating praxis," one which "posits as fundamental that the people subjected to domination must fight for their emancipation."[3]

There is no place in the liberal concept of human development for this emphasis upon practice. Whether education comes as a gift bestowed from above to those who are deprived or whether it emerges from our critical problem-posing and reflections appears irrelevant. But the key link of human development and practice puts at the center of the question "revolutionary practice"—that simultaneous changing of circumstances and human activity or self-change.

In fact, Marx introduced his concept of revolutionary practice in the very context of criticizing the idea that you can change people by giving them gifts. This was the essence of the utopian socialism of his time—that if we change the circumstances for people (for example, by creating new structures, new communities, and the like, and by inserting people into these), they will be themselves different people. And Marx said no, you are forgetting something rather important: you are forgetting really existing human beings. You are forgetting that it is *they* who change circumstances and that they change themselves in the process.

Further, who is this "we" that would change circumstances for people? This idea that we can change circumstances for people and thus change them, Marx noted, divides society into two parts—one part of which is superior to society. Indeed, is there a group of people at the top of society who will change circumstances for us? A group that knows how to build socialism for us? A group that knows enough to bestow that gift upon those whom they consider to know nothing? You are forgetting, Marx remarked, something else rather important—that "the educator must himself be educated."[4]

PRODUCTION OF HUMAN CAPACITY
AS A LABOR PROCESS

Make the key link of human development and practice our starting point and there is a simple answer to the question of how the development of human capacity occurs: we develop through all our activities. As the French Marxist Lucien Sève commented, "Every developed personality appears to us straightaway as *an enormous accumulation of the most varied acts through time*," and those acts play a central role in producing human "capacities"— "the ensemble of 'actual potentialities,' innate or acquired, to carry out any act whatever and whatever its level."[5]

Thus in all activities—both within an organized labor process as well as away from such a process—people produce in themselves the potentialities to carry out other acts that reproduce and expand their capabilities. "Every kind of consumption," Marx pointed out, "in one way or another produces human beings in some particular aspect"; thus, when "attending lectures, educating his children, developing his taste, etc.," the worker expands his capacities in different dimensions.[6] In short, the worker explicitly pursues his "own need for development" when he uses his time away from the organized workplace "for education, for intellectual development, for the fulfillment of social functions, for social intercourse, for the free play of the vital forces of his body and his mind."[7]

People engage in a labor process when they have the explicit goal of their own development and engage in purposeful activity to that end. Thus "it goes without saying," Marx commented, "that direct labour time itself cannot remain in the abstract antithesis to free time in which it appears from the perspective of bourgeois economy." What people do away from the workplace as such affects their capabilities; it allows them to enter "into the direct production process as this different subject." From this standpoint, free time can be regarded as "the production of fixed capital, this fixed capital being man himself."[8]

But people also transform themselves when their own development is *not* their preconceived goal. (In this case, it is an unintended consequence of their activities.) "The coincidence of the changing of circumstances and of human activity or self-change" is, after all, the essence of Marx's view of "the self-creation of man as a process."[9] Marx was most consistent on this point when talking about the struggles of workers against capital and how this revolutionary practice transforms "circumstances and men," expanding their capabilities and making them fit to create a new world.[10]

Marx, though, did not at all limit his view of this process of self-change to the sphere of political and economic struggle. In the very act of producing "the producers change, too, in that they bring out new qualities in themselves, develop themselves in production, transform themselves, develop new powers and new ideas, new modes of intercourse, new needs and new language."[11] The worker as outcome of his own labor, indeed, enters into

Marx's discussion in *Capital* of the labor process—there the worker "acts upon external nature and changes it, and in this way he simultaneously changes his own nature."[12]

In short, every labor process inside and outside the formal process of production (that is, every act of production, every human activity) has as its result a *joint product*—both the change in the object of labor and the change in the laborer herself.

CAPITALISM AND HUMAN DEVELOPMENT

But what about human activity under capitalist relations of production? What is the joint product that develops alongside the commodities containing surplus value that emerge from this particular labor process? How are the capacities of producers shaped by the social relations characteristic of capitalism?

One result of capitalist production is that human capacity may develop as an unintended consequence, a joint product, of capital's attempt to drive beyond all barriers to its growth. The "ceaseless striving" of capital to grow, Marx argued, is why, compared to its predecessors, the rule of capital "creates the material elements for the development of the rich individuality."[13] The daily activity of people in pre-capitalist societies—"the traditional, confined, complacent, encrusted satisfactions of present needs, and reproductions of old ways of life"—restricted the expansion of human capacities.

Capital's civilizing mission thus was to destroy these barriers to human development:

> It is destructive towards all of this, and constantly revolutionizes it, tearing down all the barriers which hem in the development of the forces of production, the expansion of needs, the all-sided development of production, and the exploitation and exchange of natural and mental forces.[14]

Similarly, capital creates *"the material elements"* for expanded human capacity insofar as it transforms the existing mode of production. Not only do new combinations of producers introduced by capital provide conditions in which the worker may go beyond "the fetters of his individuality," but the development of large-scale industry, Marx proposed, creates capital's need for "the fitness of the worker for the maximum number of different kinds of labour."[15] Indeed, Marx commented that the capitalist drive for surplus value "spurs on the development of society's productive forces, and the creation of those material conditions of production which alone can form the real basis of a higher form of society, a society in which the full and free development of every individual forms the ruling principle."[16]

However, though Marx understood that capital strives in this way toward universality, producing "this being as the most total and universal possible social product," he was very clear that capital produces its *own* barriers to the production of rich human beings.[17] Capital, recall, *only* produces for surplus value, and in crises it periodically demonstrates openly what is always true— that "instead of the proportion between production and social needs, the needs of socially developed human beings," what determines production is its profitability.[18] But this display of the limited nature of production under capital is only one example of its barrier to the production of rich human beings.

Although capital's drive for surplus value "creates material elements for the development of the rich individuality" (and "material conditions" for a higher form of society), it produces at the same time *poor* human beings. Think about the situation of workers in capitalism. Within capitalist relations of production, people are subjected to "the powerful will of a being outside them, who subjects their activity to his purpose." Everything about the capitalist relation mystifies the process of production: workers naturally don't think about the means of production as *theirs*, as the result of their labor or that of past generations of workers; rather, capitalist relations of production create in workers a "state of complete indifference, externality and alienation" in relation to those conditions of production. The combination of producers that increases social productivity appears to them as external and alien:

> The worker actually treats the social character of his work, its combination with the work of others for a common goal, as a power that is alien to him; the conditions in which this combination is realized are for him the property of another, and he would be completely indifferent to the wastage of this property if he were not himself constrained to economize on it.[19]

In short, the creative power of the worker's labor in capitalism "establishes itself as the power of capital, as an *alien power* confronting him."[20] Fixed capital, machinery, technology, all "the general productive forces of the social brain," appear as attributes of capital and as independent of workers.[21] Workers produce products that are the property of capital, which are turned against them and dominate them as capital. The world of wealth, Marx commented, faces the worker "as an alien world dominating him."

This alien world dominates the worker more and more because capital constantly creates new needs as the result of its requirement to realize the surplus value contained in commodities. For workers, producing within this relationship is a process of a "complete emptying-out," "total alienation," the "sacrifice of the human end-in-itself to an entirely external end."[22] How else but with money, the true need that capitalism creates, can we fill the vacuum? We fill the vacuum of our lives with *things*—we are driven to consume.

But that's only one way that capitalism deforms people. In *Capital*, Marx described the mutilation, the impoverishment, the "crippling of body and mind" of the worker "bound hand and foot for life to a single specialized operation" that occurs in the

division of labor characteristic of the capitalist process of manufacturing. Did the development of machinery rescue workers
under capitalism? Certainly, the potential to permit workers to
develop their capabilities was there; however, you can detect the
horror with which Marx explained how machinery provided a
technical basis for the capitalist "inversion"—how it *completed* the
"separation of the intellectual faculties of the production process
from manual labour."[23]

In this situation, head and hand become separate and hos-
tile. "Every atom of freedom, both in bodily and in intellectual
activity," is lost. "All means for the development of production
undergo a dialectical inversion," Marx indicated; "they distort
the worker into a fragment of a man," they degrade him and
"alienate from him the intellectual potentialities of the labour
process." These are just some of the distortions characteristic of
capitalist production.[24] In short, in addition to producing commodities and capital itself, the joint product of capitalist production that Marx identified in *Capital* is the fragmented, crippled human being, whose enjoyment consists in possessing and
consuming things.

Thus, while capital creates "the material elements" for rich
human beings, "this complete working-out of the human content
appears as a complete emptying-out, this universal objectification
as total alienation, and the tearing-down of all limited, one-sided
aims as sacrifice of the human end-in-itself to an entirely external
end."[25] As noted, the mystification of capital means that "capitalist production develops a working class which by education, tradition and habit looks upon the requirements of this mode of production as self-evident natural laws."[26] And, to the extent that
they do accept the logic of capital "as self-evident natural laws,"
workers are simply the products of capital—"apathetic, thoughtless, more or less well-fed instruments of production."[27] How
could anyone think that capitalism is compatible with all-around
human development?

THE SPECTER HAUNTING MARX'S *CAPITAL*

But there is an alternative to capitalism. Once we understand Marx's consistent focus upon human development, it is clear that the very premise of his *Capital* is the concept of a society in which the development of all human powers is an end in itself. The "society of free individuality, based on the universal development of individuals and on the subordination of their communal, social productivity as their social wealth" is the specter that haunts Marx's *Capital*.[28]

Can we doubt at all the presence of this other world oriented to the human end-in-itself from *Capital*'s opening sentence? We are immediately introduced to the horror of a society in which wealth appears *not* as real human wealth but rather as "an immense collection of commodities."[29] Can we doubt at all that socialism is Marx's premise when *without any logical development in this supremely logical work*, Marx suddenly evokes a society characterized *not* by the capitalist's impulse to increase the value of his capital but by "the inverse situation in which objective wealth is there to satisfy the worker's own need for development"?[30]

Excuse me, *what* "inverse situation"? Where was this ever discussed? This "inverse situation" is in fact precisely the perspective from which Marx persistently critiques capitalism. After all, he characterizes how means of production employ workers in capitalism as "this inversion, indeed this distortion, which is peculiar to and characteristic of capitalist production." But an inversion and distortion of *what*? Simply, an inversion of the "relation between dead labour and living labour" in a *different* society, one in which the results of past labor are "there to satisfy the worker's own need for development."[31]

Read *Capital* with the purpose of identifying the inversions and distortions that produce truncated human beings in capitalism and we can get a sense of Marx's idea of what is "peculiar to and characteristic of" production in that "inverse situation," socialism. We understand that all means for the development of production are *not* necessarily "means of domination and exploitation of the producers" but that this is a "distortion"—that in socialism, we would be *liberated* and not enslaved by our own products. We begin to understand the necessary conditions for producing rich human beings by considering Marx's account of their negation in capitalism.

SUBJECTS OF PRODUCTION

What are the characteristics, then, of socialist production—the circumstances that have as their joint product "the totally developed individual, for whom the different social functions are different modes of activity he takes up in turn"?[32] What kind of activities are essential to produce this rich human being whose "own realisation exists as an inner necessity, as *need*"?

Given the "dialectical inversion" peculiar to capitalist production that cripples the body and mind of the worker and alienates her from "the intellectual potentialities of the labour process," it is clear that to develop the capacities of people the producers must put an end to what Marx called in his *Critique of the Gotha Programme* "the enslaving subordination of the individual to the division of labour, and therewith also the antithesis between mental and physical labour."[33] It is no accident that Marx indicated in *Capital* that the "revolutionary ferments whose goal is the abolition of the old division of labour stand in diametrical contradiction with the capitalist form of production."[34]

Head and hand must be reunited. For the development of rich human beings, the worker must be able to call "his own muscles into play under the control of his own brain."[35] Expanding the capabilities of people requires both mental and manual activity. Not only does the combination of education with productive labor make it possible to increase the efficiency of production; this is also, as Marx pointed out in *Capital*, "the only method of producing fully developed human beings."[36] Here, then, is the way to ensure (in the words of Marx in his *Gotha Critique*) that "the productive forces have also increased with the all-around development of the individual, and all the springs of co-operative wealth flow more abundantly."[37]

Yet, more is needed than simply the combination of mental and manual labor within the sphere of production. As Mészáros indicated in his *Beyond Capital*, the "full development of the creative potentialities of the social individuals" and of the abundance flowing from their cooperation, is *only* possible in "a society in which there is no alienated command structure to impose on the individuals," only possible in a society in which "the associated producers are themselves in full control of their productive and distributive interchanges."[38] Very simply, without "intelligent direction of production" by workers, without production "under their conscious and planned control," workers cannot develop their potential as human beings because their own power becomes a power over them.[39]

In short, if the interconnection of workers in production still "confronts them, in the realm of ideas, as a plan drawn up by the capitalist, and, in practice, as his authority, as the powerful will of a being outside them," will the worker not continue to treat "the social character of his work, its combination with the work of others for a common goal, as a power alien to him"? Rather than looking upon the means of production as the conditions for the realization of his own laboring activity, will he not view these with "complete indifference, externality and alienation" and be completely indifferent to their waste if not compelled to economize on them by that power outside him?[40]

In short, it is not simply a matter of replacing capitalist authority with the plan and authority of *others* external to the workers. As in the case of the capitalist state, that "public force organized for

social enslavement, [that] engine of class despotism," the inverted
character of capitalist production cannot be used by workers for
their own goals. The "systematic and hierarchic division of
labour" characteristic of capitalist production, with its own
"trained caste" above workers—"absorbing the intelligence of the
masses and turning them against themselves in the lower places of
the hierarchy"—must be replaced with a new social form appropriate to the "all-around development of the individual."[41]

To repeat, the working class can no more use the ready-
made despotic capitalist workplace—with its "barrack-like discipline" for its own purposes than it can use the "ready-made"
capitalist *state* machinery for its own purposes. The socialist
combination of workers that increases social productivity must
be a combination that flows from the relations of the associated
producers rather than from the plan and authority of a being
outside them. As with the concept of the self-government of the
producers "at last discovered" during the Paris Commune, self-
management within production, a labor process characterized
as "the people—acting for itself by itself," is the process by
which the producers act as collective subjects who transform
themselves as they transform circumstances and make themselves fit to create a new society.[42]

The link posited here between the self-government and self-
management of the producers is not trivial. It is essential not to be
limited by *capital*'s definition of production—one that tends to
think of production as the creation of use-values that can be a
source of surplus value. Production should not be confused with
production of specific use-values: all specific products and activities are mere moments in a process of producing human beings,
the real result of social production.[43] Thus not only production of
specific material commodities (in the so-called "productive sector") but also educational and health services, household activity
(which directly nurtures the development of human beings) and
activities within the community— all these must be recognized as

integral parts of the process of producing the social beings who
enter into all these activities.[44]

As I argued in *Build It Now*:

> But, what is production? It's not something that occurs only in
> a factory or in what we traditionally identify as a workplace.
> Every activity with the goal of providing inputs into the develop-
> ment of human beings (especially those which nurture human
> development directly) must be understood as production.
> Further, the conceptions that guide production must themselves
> be produced. . . . Only through a process in which people are
> involved in making the decisions which affect them at every rel-
> evant level (i.e., their neighbourhoods, communities and society
> as a whole)—can the goals which guide productive activity be
> the goals of the people themselves. Through their involvement
> in this democratic decision making, people transform both their
> circumstances and themselves—they produce themselves as
> subjects in the new society.[45]

The implication is obvious—*every* aspect of production must
be a site for the collective decision making and variety of activity
that develops human capacities and builds solidarity among the
particular associated producers. When workers act in workplaces
and communities in conscious cooperation with others, they produce themselves as people conscious of their interdependence
and of their own collective power. The joint product of their
activity is the development of the capacities of the producers—
precisely Marx's point when he says that "when the worker coop-
erates in a planned way with others, he strips off the fetters of his
individuality, and develops the capabilities of his species."[46] In
the words of the Bolivarian Constitution, protagonism and conscious cooperation by producers is "the necessary way of achieving the involvement to ensure their complete development, both
individual and collective."

That is why Marx looked at the cooperative factories of the mid-nineteenth century as great victories. Despite the "dwarfish forms" inherent in the private efforts of individual workers that would "never transform capitalistic society" (and despite the defects we discuss in the next chapter), Marx saw the cooperative factories as an even "greater victory" for the political economy of the working class over the political economy of capital than the Ten Hours Bill.[47] Those cooperatives demonstrated in practice that combined labor on a large scale could lose its "antithetical character" and could "be carried on without the existence of a class of masters employing a class of hands." Workers, it was now revealed, do not need capitalists: "To bear fruit, the means of labour need not be monopolized as a means of dominion over, and of extortion against, the labouring man himself."[48]

Further, the cooperatives pointed to the emergence of a new relationship among the producers. Rather than embodying the goals and power of capital, the products of their activity reflected a conscious bond among the particular cooperators—one that followed from the free decision of the producers to associate. "The cooperative factories run by workers themselves" were in this respect "the first examples of the emergence of a new form."[49]

In the cooperative society based on common ownership of the means of production, the associated producers expend "their many different forms of labour-power in full self-awareness as one single social labour force."[50] And the result is the "all-around development of the individual, and [that] all the springs of cooperative wealth flow more abundantly." In short, worker management makes possible the development of the capacities of workers: the worker "strips off the fetters of his individuality, and develops the capabilities of his species." *But if workers don't manage?*

When workers don't manage, *someone else* does. The implication is clear when we recall the key link of human development and practice. If workers don't develop their capabilities through their practice, *someone else* does. This was the experience of efforts to build socialism in the twentieth century, and that experience also demonstrates that however much you may think you have banished capitalism from the house, when production is not based upon worker management, upon the relation of production of associated producers, sooner or later capitalism comes in—first, slipping in through the back door, and then marching openly through the front door.

This was certainly the case in the former Soviet Union. Workers there had "job rights." Not only was there full employment, but they also had significant protection against losing their jobs or, indeed, having their individual jobs altered in a way they didn't like. That was real job security. What Soviet workers did *not* have, though, was power to make decisions within the workplace. And they had no independent and autonomous voice: in the trade unions, which protected their individual job rights, the leadership was selected from above and principally played the role of transmission belts to mobilize the workers in production.

The results were predictable: workers were alienated, cared little about the quality of what they produced or about improving production, worked as little as possible, and used the time and energy they had left over to function in the "second" economy or informal sector. No one could possibly suggest that these relations within production tend to produce rich human beings.

There was also another effect of the denial of opportunity for workers to manage their workplaces and to develop their capabilities. Someone *else* did develop those capabilities—the enterprise managers and their staff. This was a group that maximized its income by its knowledge of production, its ability to manipulate the conditions for obtaining bonuses and its development of horizontal and vertical links and alliances. Theirs was a perspective quite different from that of workers—a perspective that rejected, among other things, job rights and stressed the rationality of a reserve army of the unemployed. Not surprisingly, the managers emerged as the capitalist class of the Soviet Union.[51]

Worker management of state-owned productive units is a necessary condition for producing rich human beings. *But is that enough?* In 1949, the Yugoslav leadership explicitly rejected the Soviet model—particularly in relation to the position of workers. They described the Soviet model as state capitalism and bureaucratic despotism, and they argued that the bureaucracy in the Soviet Union had become a new class. State ownership of the means of production, the Yugoslav leaders declared, was only a *precondition* of socialism.

For socialism, you need socialist relations of production—self-management. "From now on," Marshal Tito, president of Yugoslavia, noted in introducing the Law on Workers' Self-Management in 1950, state ownership of the means of production "will gradually be transformed into a higher form of ownership, socialist ownership. State property is the lowest form of social property and not the highest as thought by the leaders of the USSR."[52] Without worker management, the Yugoslav leaders insisted, there is no socialism.

But we have to ask, what was the *goal* of worker management in Yugoslavia? Doesn't that matter? Is the nature of production and the nature of those produced within the process of production independent of the goal of production? Is state ownership of the means of production and worker management *sufficient* to produce rich human beings? The question brings us to the third side of the socialist triangle.

3. The Solidarian Society

Let us return to the concept of the good society—a society that we think of as good, as one in which we would like to live and to which we think everyone has a right. Ensuring that our social heritage, the result of past social labor, belongs to everyone rather than to a limited group is essential. So, too, is the ability in our productive activity to develop our potential through worker and community management—as opposed to that "systematic and hierarchic division of labour" characteristic of capitalist production, with its own "trained caste" above workers—"absorbing the intelligence of the masses and turning them against themselves in the lower places of the hierarchy." *But, productive activity for what purpose?* Doesn't that matter in the society we want?

In particular, what is the place of self-interest in our activity? For Adam Smith, self-interest was essential because he argued that no one can expect help from others based upon benevolence alone. A person is more likely to get what he wants from others "if he can interest their self-love in his favour, and show them that it is for their own advantage to do for him what he requires of them." In short, we contract with each other: "Give me that which I want, and you shall have this which you want." That is how we satisfy our needs:

It is not from the benevolence of the butcher, the brewer, or the baker that we expect our dinner, but from their regard to their own interest. We address ourselves, not to their humanity but to their self-love, and never talk to them of our own necessities but of their advantages.[1]

THE SELF-INTEREST OF OWNERS

What kind of society is this? For Marx, it is one in which the focus is not upon "the association of man with man, but on the separation of man from man." It begins, in short, from the premise that we are *separate*, that the community of human beings is at its core a relationship of separate property owners. Society as such, Marx commented in 1843, "appears as a framework external to the individuals, as a restriction of their original independence. The sole bond holding them together is natural necessity, needs and private interest, the preservation of their property and their egoistic selves."[2] This is how political economy views society, he proposed—it "starts out from the *relation of man to man* as that of *property owner to property owner.*"[3]

Implicit in our relation of property owners is the possibility of exchanging our property. Why does that take place? As Smith noted, exchange occurs when it is in our individual self-interest. In this process of exchanging our products, Marx observed, "I have produced for myself and not for you, just as you have produced for yourself and not for me." In other words, I am not producing for you as another human being. "That is to say, our production is not man's production for man as a man, i.e., it is not *social* production." And, of course, "since our exchange is a selfish one, on your side as on mine, and since the selfishness of each seeks to get the better of that of the other, we necessarily seek to deceive each other." We struggle against each other, and "the victor is the one who has more energy, force, insight, or adroitness."[4]

What happens, in contrast, when we *do* relate to each other as human beings? If our relationship is that of being part of the human family, then if you have a need I would want to help. When we relate as *owners*, however, your need does not induce me to help you as another human being. On the contrary, your need gives me *power* over you. Your needs make you dependent upon me: "Far from being the *means* which would give you *power* over my production, they are instead the *means* for giving me power over you." At the same time, my needs give you power over me. We struggle against each other because we are, in fact, separate self-seekers. And, in this social relation of commodity producers, we don't look upon our productive activity as an expression of ourselves and as a joy. To secure what I need, I *must* produce for you. Accordingly, my activity is forced. It is a "torment," toil and trouble, "a *forced* activity and one imposed on me only through an *external* fortuitous need, *not* through an *inner, essential* one." [5]

What kind of people are produced in this relationship that begins with "the separation of man from man"? Very clearly, the kind of people who *remain* alienated from each other, from our activity and from our own products. Indeed, we are the property of our own products, we are in "mutual thralldom to the object." And there is no obvious escape from inside this relation. If I were to say to you that I have a need, "it would be recognised and felt as being a request, an entreaty, and therefore a *humiliation*, and consequently uttered with a feeling of shame, of degradation." At your end, "it would be regarded as *impudence* or *lunacy* and rejected as such." The only language with which we can converse in this relationship that seems to provide dignity is the "estranged language of material values," and what is rational for us as individuals is to produce exchange values. [6]

Marx never moved away from this view of the exchange relation. In the *Grundrisse*, he wrote that in exchange, despite "the all-around dependence of the producers on one another," those producers are separate and isolated; there is "the total isolation of their private interests from one another." What exists, accordingly, is "the connection of mutually indifferent persons." And "their mutual interconnection—here appears as something alien to them, autonomous, as a thing." In the "reciprocal and all-sided dependence of individuals who are indifferent to one another," the connection of people exists as a relation "external to the individuals and independent of them"; it is, in fact, a power over them.

We have an overwhelming need, the "real need" produced in this system—*money*. We must transform our products and our activities into money, which gives us "social power" over the activities of others; money here is "our bond with society," and we are dominated and subordinated by this connection. We must function in the market. Our own social product, this connection of "mutually indifferent individuals," drives us and gives us impulse. The market is our connection as mutually indifferent individuals, and it is a power over us.[7] The contrast between this relation of people who relate to each other as separate property owners and one in which our activity is "the offspring of association," that is, one in which our activity is based upon the premise of a community, could not be sharper for Marx. [8]

SELF-INTEREST IN THE COOPERATIVES

And this is the context to understand Marx's critique of the cooperative factories that emerged in the mid-nineteenth century. Cooperative factories, as we saw in the last chapter, demonstrated that workers do not need capitalists; they were in this respect a great advance, "the first examples of the emergence of a new form." But that new form was emerging "within the old form." The cooperatives were reproducing "all the defects of the existing system." They did not go beyond profit-seeking and competition. Though they combined workers on a new basis and abolished the

opposition between capital and labor, this cooperative production remained an isolated system "based upon individual and
antagonistic interests," one in which the associated workers had
"become their own capitalist," using the means of production to
"valorize their own labour." [9]

Focus upon cooperatives as the answer for workers was a
"sham and a snare." In part, it was because they were "dwarfish
forms" and the private efforts of individual workers would "never
transform capitalistic society":

> To convert social production into one large and harmonious sys-
> tem of free and co-operative labour, *general social changes* are
> wanted, *changes of the general conditions of society*, never to be
> realised save by the transfer of the organised forces of society,
> viz., the state power, from capitalists and landlords to the pro-
> ducers themselves.[10]

But there was another key element to Marx's criticism of the
cooperatives. A cooperative society based upon common ownership of the means of production was essential. *But not on the basis
of the market and self-interest.* The cooperatives had to go *beyond*
the "defects of the existing system." Rather than being "based
upon individual and antagonistic interests," development of this
harmonious system of associated labor required that the cooperatives themselves had to *cooperate*: "United co-operative societies
are to regulate national production upon a common plan, thus
taking it under their own control."[11] In this case, associated producers would expend "their many different forms of labour-
power *in full self-awareness* as one single social labour force."[12]

For Marx, that harmonious system of associated labor was
inconsistent with market relations and self-interest:

> The veil is not removed from the countenance of the social life-
> process, i.e. the process of material production, until it becomes

production by freely associated men, and stands under their conscious and planned control.[13]

SELF-INTEREST IN SOCIALISM

Marx was very clear in his *Critique of the Gotha Programme* in describing socialism as it emerges from capitalist society as "in every respect, economically, morally and intellectually, still stamped with the birthmarks of the old society from whose womb it emerges." Characteristic of socialism as it emerges was a particular "defect"—an "inevitable" defect. And that defect is revealed by the continued existence of an exchange relation: "Accordingly, the individual producer receives back from society—after the deductions have been made—exactly what he gives to it." It is an exchange not of commodities—"the producers do not exchange their products"—but it is an exchange of one's labor with society: "The same amount of labour which he has given to society in one form he gets back in another."

"Give me that which I want, and you shall have this which you want." This relation is an exchange between an owner and the one who owns the use-values he desires, an exchange of equivalents. "The same principle prevails as in the exchange of commodity-equivalents: a given amount of labour in one form is exchanged for an equal amount of labour in another form." What we see here is the continuation of "*bourgeois right*"—the claims of individual producers upon society's output are determined *not by their membership in society* but, rather, are "*proportional* to the labour they supply."[14] This "defect" was a defect in the relation of distribution—a relation often described as distribution in accordance with work (or contribution).

Yet, as Marx pointed out, it was a "mistake" of the Gotha Programme to stress "so-called *distribution*." Relations of distribution, after all, are only the "reverse side" of relations of production; they cannot be treated "as independent of the mode of production." *So precisely what is the relation of production that generates this particular distribution rule?* (Why is this question not asked despite all the invocation of the phrase "bourgeois right"?) The relation of production that underlies this specific relation of distribution involves *production by private owners of labor power*.[15] Despite the common ownership of the means of production, labor power remains here private property:

> The capitalist mode of production . . . rests on the fact that the material conditions of production are in the hands of non-workers in the form of property in capital and land, while the masses are only owners of the personal condition of production, of labour power.[16]

Common ownership of the "material conditions of production" is thus only a *partial* passage beyond the "narrow horizon of bourgeois right." Insofar as producers relate to each other as the "owners of the personal condition of production, of labourpower," each producer (group of producers) demands a *quid pro quo* for the expenditure of her (their) activity. Each seeks to maximize income for a given quantity of labor (or to minimize labor for a given income). "Give me that which I want, and you shall have this which you want," after all, implies its opposite: if I don't get the equivalent, you shall not have what *you* want. As separate owners of labor power, the interests of society do not guide the activity of producers.

And what is the effect of this defect of private ownership of labor-power and self-interest? *Inequality*. Marx pointed out that an exchange of equivalents by which a producer is entitled to receive "the same amount of labour which he has given to society" is a "*right of inequality*" that "tacitly recognizes unequal individual endowment and thus productive capacity as natural privileges." The only thing that matters in such a social relation is how much labor an individual has contributed. But how could this be accepted as a just relationship in a socialist society? *It is an entirely one-sided perspective!* Unequal individuals are considered, Marx noted, "from one *definite* side only, for instance, in the present case, are regarded *only as workers* and nothing more is seen in them, everything else being ignored." [17]

Just like the political economy that Marx criticized in his earliest writings, the conception of distribution according to contribution looks at the producer "only as a *worker*. . . . It does not consider him when he is not working, as a human being."[18] Unlike many of his followers, this was a perspective Marx always rejected. Indeed, precisely because differences in ability imply no differences in needs, *The German Ideology* argued that "the false tenet, based upon existing circumstances, 'to each according to his abilities,' must be changed, insofar as it relates to enjoyment in its narrow sense, into the tenet, '*to each according to his need*'; in other words, a *different form* of activity, of labour, does not justify *inequality*, confers no *privileges* in respect of possession and enjoyment."[19]

As we can see, Marx was very critical of the inequality that flows from this "defect"; however, he vastly *understated* the inequality that emerges as the result of the self-oriented activity manifested in the social relation of exchange. People differ in far more ways than the "individual endowments" to which he pointed. Remember, as noted in chapter 1, producers *also* possess different particular means of production. And, insofar as those means of production are possessed by self-seeking producers (even with common ownership and worker management), the result of this differential access to particular means of production will tend to be that some owners of labor power are able to secure benefits from which other members of society are excluded—that is, for the rule of distribution to become "to each according to his contribution and that of the means of production he possesses."

SELF-INTEREST AND YUGOSLAV
SELF-MANAGEMENT

The experience of Yugoslavia is interesting because this case of state-owned industry and legally mandated worker management demonstrates the effects of reproducing "all the defects of the existing system." Having rejected the Soviet model, Yugoslavia began in 1950 to introduce worker management in state industry.[20] It was a real experiment. Would worker management of state-owned industries succeed?

In introducing the Law on Workers' Self-Management, Marshal Tito pointed out that many people worried that "the workers will not be able to master the complicated techniques of management of factories and other enterprises." His answer, though, was that "in the very process of management, in the continuous process of work and management, all the workers will gain the necessary experience. They will get acquainted not only with the work process, but also with all the problems of their enterprises. Only through practice will workers be able to learn."[21]

Certainly, the extreme alienation characteristic of the Soviet workplace was not to be found. Yugoslav workers did identify with their enterprises, and Yugoslavia was viewed as a great success story as it industrialized and introduced modern technology. Further, large numbers *did* learn much about the problems of their enterprises—especially because there was a principle of rotation on the workers' councils both at the enterprise and shop levels. But they learned much less than Tito and other leaders had anticipated at the beginning.

What had happened? One major problem is that there was not a sustained effort to educate workers in the workplace as to how to run their enterprises. So the result was that the distinction between thinking and doing remained. Although they had the power to decide upon critical questions like investments, marketing, and production, the workers' councils didn't feel they had the competence to make these decisions—compared with the managers and technical experts. Thus they tended to rubber-stamp proposals that came from management.

The councils, on the other hand, spent a lot of time discussing things that they did feel competent to judge—like the fairness of relative incomes within the enterprise. Why weren't the workers real self-managers? A very important part of the problem is the context in which these self-managed enterprises existed: they functioned in the market and were driven by one thing—*self-interest*. In every enterprise, the goal was to maximize income per member of the individual enterprise. Since the managers as well as workers benefited from the success of the enterprise, it was accepted that they all had a common interest in making money.

Thus there was solidarity among members of individual enterprises, but that solidarity did not extend to workers in different, competing enterprises (or to society in general). As Che Guevara had noted in 1959, each firm was "engaged in violent struggle with its competitors over prices and quality." He commented that this was a real danger because this competition could "introduce factors that distort what the socialist spirit should presumably be."[22]

A key question is, then, worker management for *what*? If the goal of worker management is cooperation among a specific group of producers for the purpose of maximizing income per worker, then *who is the Other*? The answer is *other* groups of workers who are competing, producers who are selling required inputs, members of society who are your market or who assert a claim upon your means of production or upon the results of your labor, those who would tax you, the state—indeed, *everyone else*.

Not surprisingly, it was argued that taxation was exploitation by a Stalinist state. Under the demands from self-managed enterprises for increased decision-making power, the state retreated significantly from taxation and investment. The argument advanced was that continuation of petty tutelage and restrictions on enterprise autonomy left producers in a wage-labor relation. So, with the theoretical logic that by being able to make their own production and investment decisions these enterprises with workers councils as their legal governing bodies would expand the capacities of workers, Yugoslavia moved increasingly to a market-led economy.

With this shift to the market, though, inequality grew— inequality between firms in one industry, between industries, between town and country, and between republics. And another kind of inequality emerged: these self-managed enterprises used the funds no longer taxed away by the state (supporting extensive development) for machine-intensive investments that could generate more income without adding more members to their collective. Not surprisingly, unemployment was high because people coming from the countryside couldn't find jobs, so they went to countries in western Europe as "guest workers."

This last inequality revealed a significant problem in the real meaning of social property. While these enterprises were legally property of the state and were viewed as social property, there was differential access to the means of production. Some workers had access to much better means of production than others, and the unemployed obviously had access to *no* means of production.[23] Given the self-interest that dominated the activity of self-managed enterprises, all members of the society did not have equal access to and did not gain equal benefits from those commonly owned means of production.

Growing inequalities, in short, were the product of monopolies—the ability to exclude others from particular means of production. Rather than social property, what existed was *group property*. "Although social property may be legally established," the leading Yugoslav economist Branko Horvat noted, "this difference in incomes or the relative size of nonlabor income in privileged industries reflects the degree of privatization of social property."[24] While new measures and constitutional changes were introduced to strengthen workers against what was described as a "techno-bureaucracy" ruling over expanded reproduction, those measures did not challenge the new productive relation that had been strengthened by market relations—group ownership of these enterprises.

Indeed, the failure to reverse the existing pattern reflected the entrenched power of the group property relation—a relation that only on its surface was one of worker management. It was the managers and technical experts in these enterprises who understood marketing and selling commodities; it was the managers and technical experts who knew about investments, about placing the funds of the enterprises in banks and establishing links with other enterprises, creating mergers, and so forth. Workers didn't know these things—they knew that they were dependent upon the experts.

The Yugoslavian case demonstrates that the existence of workers councils—even with the legal power to make all decisions—is not the same as worker management; and focus upon the self-interest of workers in individual enterprises is not the same as a focus upon the interest of the working class as a whole. State-owned enterprises had workers councils—but the division between thinking and doing continued. In the absence of worker management, someone else managed. In the absence of workers developing their capacities, someone else does. In the end, the managers emerged as capitalists, leaving the workers as wage-laborers.

SELF-INTEREST AS AN INFECTION IN SOCIALISM

Even with state ownership of the means of production and the institution of workers councils for the purpose of worker management, an overwhelming emphasis upon self-interest undermines the development of socialism as an organic system. When maximizing income is the goal, the Yugoslav experience shows that it may be logical to rely upon experts who promise to take workers to that goal; the result will be to undermine worker management and to ensure that workers do not develop their potential. Further, when one's labor power is viewed as property that requires an equivalent, the resulting inequality (and related jealousy and antagonisms) work against the development and deepening of solidarity in society and against a focus upon the needs of people within society. Finally, when differential possession or differential development of capacities (neither of which imply antagonism in themselves) are combined with self-interest and self-orientation to produce the belief in and the desire for privileged entitlement, the tendency is toward the disintegration of the common ownership of the means of production. *Self-orientation infects all sides of the socialist triangle.*

Should we be surprised at this? Individual and antagonistic interests, competition, profit seeking, maximizing material self-interest—how can this be part of a new socialist society? It is precisely the point made by Che in his *Man and Socialism in Cuba*:

> The pipe dream that socialism can be achieved with the help of the dull instruments left to us by capitalism (the commodity as the economic cell, individual material interest as the lever, etc.) can lead into a blind alley. And you wind up there after having travelled a long distance with many crossroads, and it is hard to figure out just where you took the wrong turn.[25]

It *is* a dead end; it is a "blind alley" precisely because this reproduces "all the defects of the existing system." To build the new society, as Che knew, it is necessary, simultaneous with new material foundations, to build new socialist human beings. But what kind of people are built when self-interest is the dominant principle? What are the joint products of that process?

PRODUCING FOR THE NEEDS OF OTHERS

Marx's rejection of people relating to each other as separate self-seekers was always based upon an alternative—individuals who develop their qualities within a human society. In contrast to the existence of a person within "civil society, in which he acts as a private individual, regards other men as a means, degrades himself into a means," Marx posited a "*communal being.*"[26] In contrast to "the separation of man from man," he stressed the "association of man with man"; in contrast to seeing others as "the *barrier*" to one's own freedom, the alternative was seeing other people as "the *realisation* of his own freedom."[27] The alternative to the "egoistic man, . . . man separated from other men and from the community," was for Marx always the social human being.

What is that alternative? If you have a need, does that give me power over you? Or does it stimulate me to want to help you? The first is the case Marx explored in which two people confront each other as separate owners, as owners of the products of their labor. Its premise is their separation, their alienation, their atomism—in a word, the absence of community, and that is what is reproduced. In contrast, the second case begins from the premise of our association, our conscious bond. The result of this productive activity, the "offspring of association," is entirely different in this case.

"Let us suppose we had carried out production as human beings." In this case, producing as members of a human family, if I produce consciously for your need, I know my work is valuable, I know that I am satisfying your need, and I gain from this.[28] "In my individual activity," Marx commented, "I would have directly *confirmed* and *realised* my true nature, my *human* nature, my *communal nature.*" My work in this relationship is a "*free manifestation of life*, hence an *enjoyment of life*"; this activity, to use a term Marx employed later, is indeed "life's prime want." And, in this way, we not only produce ourselves—we also produce our relation, our connection as members of a human society.[29]

What is so obvious here is the joint product characteristic of this relation—in producing directly and consciously for others, we not only satisfy the needs of others but we also produce ourselves as rich human beings. This theme of the realization of human potential only by producing within and for others in a community permeates Marx's early writing. In this new society, he proposed, there is "*communal* activity and *communal* enjoyment—i.e., activity and enjoyment manifested and affirmed in *actual* direct *association* with other men." Here, "man's *need* has become a *human* need" to the extent to which "the *other* person as a person has become for him a need—the extent to which he in his individual existence is at the same time a social being."[30]

This communal society, once developed, "produces man in this entire richness of his being—produces the *rich* man *profoundly endowed with all the senses*—as its enduring reality."[31] But what does that require? It depends "on whether we live in circumstances that allow all-round activity and thereby the full development of all our potentialities," and that is only possible when "the world which stimulates the real development of the abilities of the individual is under the control of the individuals themselves, as the communists desire."[32]

In the *Grundrisse*, Marx stated explicitly that the premise for producing as social beings and thereby producing ourselves as rich human beings is *community*—the association of producers within society. In contrast to the "mutually indifferent persons" who are the premise of the exchange relation, here "a communal production, communality, is presupposed as the basis of production. The labour of the individual is posited from the outset as social labour."[33] The solidarian society, in short, is the presupposition for productive activity consciously undertaken for the needs of others. The "communal character," the "*social character*," of our activity is presupposed, and thus there is an exchange not of exchange values but of "activities, determined by communal needs and communal purposes."[34]

Begin from this presupposed communal society, and social production that is "directly social," which is "the offspring of association," follows. Begin with the communal character of our activity, and the product of our activity is "a communal, general product from the outset." Thus the distribution of products follows: the exchange of our activities "would from the outset include the participation of the individual in the communal world of products."[35] Begin with communality, and "instead of a division of labour, . . . there would take place an organization of labour."[36] Here, where there is a "free exchange among individuals who are associated on the basis of common appropriation and control of the means of production," is the basis for the development of rich human beings. Here, in this solidarian society, Marx envisioned "free individuality, based on the universal development of individuals and on their subordination of their communal, social productivity as their social wealth."[37]

As Mészáros pointed out in his *Beyond Capital*, "The lines of demarcation between the communal system on the one hand, and systems dominated by the division of labour and the corresponding value-relation on the other, could not be drawn more emphatically than they are here" in the *Grundrisse*.[38] It was Marx's discussion referred to above that Mészáros drew on for what he called the "Archimedean point"—"the nature of *exchange* in the communal system of production and consumption." This, Mészáros noted, was "the historically novel character of the communal system"—"its practical orientation towards the *exchange of activities*, and not simply of *products*."[39] And, as indicated earlier, it was his reading of Mészáros's analysis that influenced and led Hugo Chávez to proclaim in 2005:

> The Point of Archimedes, this expression taken from the wonderful book of Istvan Mészáros, a communal system of production and of consumption—that is what we are creating, we know we are building this. We have to create a communal system of

production and consumption, a new system.... Let us remember that Archimedes said: "You give me an intervention point and I will move the world." This is the point from which to move the world today.[40]

This point is indeed essential. In this social relation, where the associated producers consciously engage in productive activity for the needs of the community, there is a continuous process of development of the capabilities of the producers. This simultaneous process of the changing of circumstances and self-change creates rich human beings as the joint product of productive activity. Grasping this point gives particular meaning to the concept of "from each according to his ability"—the first half of what Mészáros calls "the orienting principle of socialist accountancy." Production according to ability means "on the basis of the *full development of the creative potentialities of the social individuals*"; and this is the precondition for "meeting the requirements of the second half, i.e. the satisfaction of the individuals' needs." Without that first half, "the second half has no chance of being taken seriously."

However, as Mészáros points out, there has been a tendency to focus solely upon the second half of "the socialist regulating principle": "The first half is usually, and tellingly, forgotten."[41] It is not only the conscious adversaries of socialism, however, who ignore the essential meaning of "from each according to his ability." If you do not look at both sides of this principle, you are likely to ignore its *premise*—the solidarian society, where "universally developed individuals, whose social relations, as their own communal relations, are hence also subordinated to their own communal control."[42]

What happens if you do not consciously and continuously build that premise, the solidarian society? You are left with two things. One is the empty hope that someday people will change (if only productive forces are developed sufficiently). The other is the infection that, sooner or later, takes its toll on the body.

PART 2

Building the Socialist Triangle

4. The Being and Becoming of an Organic System

Part 2 of this book, "Building the Socialist Triangle," takes up the question of the building of socialism, the becoming of socialism as an organic system. This chapter and chapter 5, "The Concept of a Socialist Transition," explore the subject theoretically and in the abstract. The two chapters provide a foundation for the following two chapters—"Making a Path to Socialism" and "Building a Socialist Mode of Regulation." There, we proceed to consider the question of building socialism *concretely* with the identification of specific steps along a possible path. But first, let us consider the interdependence of the three sides of the socialist triangle that have been the subject of the preceding three chapters.

SOCIALISM AS AN ORGANIC SYSTEM

The three sides of the "socialist triangle" are members of a whole. As parts of a "structure in which all the elements coexist simultaneously and support one another," they mutually interact. "This is the case with every organic whole."[1] Therein is the "universal, all-sided, *vital*, connection of everything with everything" that Lenin found in Hegel, the whole composed of various elements that "stand to one another in a necessary connection arising out of the nature of the organism."[2] Consider those three sides:

1. Social ownership of the means of production is critical within this structure because it is the only way to ensure that our communal, social productivity is directed to the free development of all rather than used to satisfy the private goals of capitalists, groups of producers, or state bureaucrats. But this concerns more than our current activity. Social ownership of our social heritage, the results of past social labor, is an assertion that all living human beings have the right to the full development of their potential—to real wealth, the development of human capacity. In particular, we need to recognize that "the worker's own need for development" is not limited to particular categories of producers or regions of the world. "The free development of each is the condition for the free development of all."

2. Social production organized by workers builds new relations among producers—relations of cooperation and solidarity. It allows workers to end "the crippling of body and mind" and the loss of "every atom of freedom, both in bodily and in intellectual activity," that comes from the separation of head and hand. As long as workers are prevented from developing their capacities by combining thinking and doing in the workplace, they remain alienated and fragmented human beings whose enjoyment consists in possessing and consuming things. Organization of production by workers is thus a condition for the full development of the producers, for the development of their capabilities—a condition for the production of rich human beings.

3. Satisfaction of communal needs and purposes as the goal of productive activity means that, instead of interacting as separate and indifferent individuals, we function as members of a community. Rather than looking upon our own capacity as our property and as a means of securing as much as possible in an exchange, we start from the recognition of our common humanity and, thus, we understand the importance of conditions in which everyone is able to develop her full potential. When our productive activity is oriented to the needs of others, it both builds solidarity among people and produces socialist human beings.

These three sides of the socialist triangle are mutually dependent and support one another. Social ownership of the means of production is a necessary condition for worker management and production for the needs of the community. In the absence of social ownership, the character of production and production decisions will not stress the joint product of socialist production—the development of rich human beings. Further, in its focus on the entitlement to the fruits of our social heritage, social ownership supports the development of solidarity based upon recognition of our common humanity and thus the development of communal institutions (such as communal councils and workers councils) in order to make communality real.

In its turn, worker and community management ensures that decisions are not conceived and executed through a "systematic and hierarchic division of labour" but rather are democratic, participatory, and protagonistic. For the means of production to remain social property, it is essential to prevent the emergence of a "trained caste" above workers, "absorbing the intelligence of the masses" and developing the capacity to rule production in place of workers. Through worker management, the producers transform themselves and develop qualitatively different needs; they express themselves through their collective productive activity rather than by possessing things and thus create the conditions for development of a solidarian society.

Finally, productive activity oriented toward communal needs and purposes has as its condition the development of communality. Without this focus upon the community, production tends to be self-oriented in its character and exists as a *means* rather than as an expression of one's capabilities and self. Communality guards against worker-managers viewing their labor power as property and as the basis of an *exchange* with society, and it checks a tendency to treat social property as group property. By stressing the principle that the free development of each is the condition for the free development of all, the solidarian society insists upon the existence of democratic, participatory and protagonistic institutions that ensure for all members of society "their complete development, both individual and collective."

The socialist triangle is a system of reproduction. Its premises are results of the system, and its products are social ownership of the means of production, social production organized by workers, and a solidarian orientation to communal needs and purposes. Yet the very interdependence of these three specific elements suggests that realization of each element depends upon the existence of the other two. Without production for social needs, no real social property; without social property, no worker decision making oriented toward society's needs; without worker decision making, no transformation of people and their needs. In socialism as an organic system, "every economic relation presupposes every other in its [socialist] economic form, and everything posited is thus also a presupposition; this is the case with every organic system."[3]

However, there is a very big difference between an organic system, one which produces its own premises and thus rests upon its own foundations, and the "*becoming*" of such a system. We will never understand Marx's conception of socialism or what he had to say about economic systems if we don't grasp the essential dis-

tinction between the "becoming" of a system and its "being"—
that is, the distinction between the historical emergence of a particular form of society and the nature of that society *once it has
developed upon its own foundations.*

THE BECOMING OF A NEW SYSTEM

An organic system does not drop from the sky:

> It must be kept in mind that the new forces of production and
> relations of production do not develop out of nothing, nor drop
> from the sky, nor from the womb of the self-positing Idea; but
> from within and in antithesis to the existing development of pro-
> duction and the inherited, traditional relations of property.[4]

A new system never produces its own premises at the outset.
Rather, when a new system emerges, it necessarily *inherits* premises from the old. Its premises and presuppositions are "historic"
ones, premises produced outside the system. And insofar as those
historic premises are from outside the system, they cannot be a
basis for understanding an organic system "in which all the elements coexist simultaneously and support one another."

For example, Marx noted that if you want to understand the
modern city, you don't do it by discussing the flight of serfs to the
cities. This is "one of the *historic* conditions and presuppositions
of urbanism [but]... not a *condition,* not a moment of the reality
of developed cities." Similarly, let's not talk about things like how
"the earth made the transition from a liquid sea of fire and vapour
to its present form." Let's talk about the earth and capitalism
now—not those "presuppositions of their becoming which are
suspended in their being."

The historic presuppositions of capitalism took many forms—
among which were individual savings acquired from various

sources. However, the dependence of capitalism upon original savings, Marx stressed, belongs "to the *history of its formation*, but in no way to its *contemporary* history, i.e. not to the real system of the mode of production ruled by it."[5] Once capitalism exists, then capital "itself, on the basis of its own reality, posits the conditions for its realization." In short, you have real capital when capital produces its own premises, when it no longer rests upon historic presuppositions. "These presuppositions, which originally appeared as conditions of its becoming—and hence could not spring from its *action as capital*—now appear as results of its own realization, reality, as *posited by it—not as conditions of its arising but as results of its presence.*"

In short, to understand capitalism as a system, we must look at how the system is reproduced, how it "creates its own presuppositions . . . by means of its own production process." We look at how capital "no longer proceeds from presuppositions in order to become, but rather it is itself presupposed, and proceeds from itself to create the conditions of its maintenance and growth."[6] That, as we have seen, is how Marx proceeded—by examining capitalism as an organic system and by demonstrating that capital is the result of the exploitation of workers and is the workers' own product turned against them. Once he had identified the essential elements in capitalist relations of production as capital and wage labor, then he could focus upon the preconditions for the *initial* emergence of each. *Theory, in short, guides the historical inquiry.* Our method, Marx noted, "indicates the points where historical investigation must enter in"; understanding the nature of capitalism as an organic system "point(s) towards a past lying behind this system."[7]

But see, Marx stressed, how bourgeois economists obscured the distinct nature of capital by "formulating the conditions of its becoming as the conditions of its contemporary realization; i.e., presenting the moments in which the capitalist still appropriates as not-capitalist—because he is still becoming—as the very conditions in which he appropriates as *capitalist*."[8] See how this completely distorts the nature of capitalism. By treating capital as if it *remains* based upon historic presuppositions like individual savings, the capitalist relation of production (and, thus, capital's dependence upon exploitation of the wage-laborer) disappears. *This is why Marx explicitly distinguished between the accumulation of capital within capitalism as a system and the "original accumulation"—and why the former must come first in our analysis.*

If we fail to distinguish between the being and the becoming of an organic system, we don't understand the elements in the *completed* system. For example, there is an essential difference between money as it emerges historically and all the sides of money within capitalism as an organic system, and the same distinction is true of the commodity. Stated another way, when we consider the elements *historically*, we are looking at the elements in their flawed and defective state—where they are not *yet* produced in their appropriate form. "How, indeed," Marx asked in 1847, "could the single logical formula of movement, of sequence, of time, explain the structure of society, in which all relations coexist simultaneously and support one another?"[9]

Every new system as it emerges is inevitably defective: it is "in every respect, economically, morally and intellectually, still stamped with the birthmarks of the old society." This understanding is at the core of a dialectical perspective. As Hegel put it, the "new world is perfectly realized as little as the new-born child"; it realizes its potential "when those previous shapes and forms . . . are developed anew again, but developed and shaped within this new medium, and with the meaning they have thereby acquired."[10] Marx understood such development as the process of *becoming*—"the process of becoming this totality forms a moment of its process, of its development." And how does this development occur? "Its development to its totality consists precisely in subordinating all elements of society to itself, or in creating out of it the organs which it still lacks. This is historically how it becomes a totality."[11]

How *precisely* does a new system become? Beginning with the defects it inherits, those characteristics of the old society, *how does it subordinate all elements of society to itself and create the organs it still lacks* in order to rest upon its own foundations? How does it develop into the organic system in which all its premises are results of the system? Marx had very little to say about this question in general. However, he did write *Capital*. So, what can we learn from his examination of the becoming of *capitalism*?

THE BECOMING OF CAPITALISM

The Subordinated Social Relation

Marx's story about the development of capitalist relations of production begins with the existence of a subordinated social relation. Although one aspect of the capitalist relation, the orientation toward securing additional value through the buying and selling of commodities (M-C-M'), existed in many societies, the commodities traded were produced under slave, feudal, petty craft, or peasant productive relations, and this merchant activity was largely subordinate to those relations. And the same was true of those who lent money for the purpose of securing more money—their activity occurred outside production itself.

The Rupture in Property Rights

With the separation of independent peasant producers from their land (through enclosures and the challenge to their rights to the land), those producers had to gain access to those (or any) means of production through a new relation. This was not, however, the only rupture in property rights that would serve ultimately as a precondition for capitalist relations—people who were unfree (such as slaves and serfs) became the owners of "the personal condition of production, of labour-power" and now had the ability to sell that labor power as a commodity.

The combination of these ruptures provided a basis for what Marx called the original (or primitive) accumulation of capital—a body of legally free producers separated from the means of production was created.[12] These ruptures were reinforced by the other side of this accumulation—not only the concentration of the means of production (land) in the hands of those looking to the market for the expansion of value but also the acquisition of large sums of money based in part upon force (for example, slavery) and upon the expansion of pre-capitalist social relations (such as the slave trade and speculation in state debt). Those who owned the means of production and oriented toward the expansion of value (M-C-M') now potentially could determine the character of production, to introduce capitalist relations of production.

Yet, though the rupture in property relations was a necessary historical precondition for the classical case Marx described, it was not a *sufficient* condition for the emergence of capitalist productive relations. True, there was a new distribution of endowments—the separation of producers from the means of production at one pole of society and, at the other pole, the concentration of those conditions of labor in the shape of capital. However, there was still an *alternative* to the sale of labor power to capitalists—producers could *rent* means of production from their owners (an obvious alternative in agriculture). Thus more than this rupture in property relations was required for capitalist productive relations.

The Emergence of New Relations of Production

Also essential was that those propertyless producers "be compelled to sell themselves voluntarily."[13] Only in situations where those who owned the means of production were able to ensure that producers would work under their direction and control and, further, where they themselves would hold property rights in the product produced did capitalist relations of production emerge. Even when the means of production "possess an independent existence" alongside the producer, "the latter is not yet subsumed into the process of capital"—this is a pre-capitalist situation that persists so long as "capital does not seize possession of production."[14]

In short, even with the new set of property rights, it was still possible that the new legal owners would not alter the relations of production. *The new path occurred, then, only when those who had property rights seized "possession of production."* Now they were in the position to hire wage laborers, to subordinate and exploit them within production in order to achieve their goal and to reproduce their conditions of existence. Yet this too was not enough to ensure the reproduction of capitalist relations of production.

In the absence of the development of the specifically capitalist mode of production, this process of reproduction was inherently unstable and sensitive to shocks or changes in the economic environment. Initially, to secure surplus value and to accumulate capital, capitalists did not alter the preexisting mode of production they inherited. Rather, they turned their efforts to ensuring that they got more work from their workers—by disciplining them, intensifying work, extending the workday. By securing absolute surplus value in this way, capitalists could maintain themselves as capitalists and continue the capitalist process of production; and the workers' lack of property rights in the products they produced, along with wages that allowed them only to maintain themselves and their families, meant that those workers would remain separated from the means of production. As long as conditions were favorable, this formal subsumption of labor under capital permitted the reproduction of the premise for capitalist production.

The Development of a Specific Mode of Production

But the reproduction of capitalist relations was tenuous as long as "the subordination of labour to capital was only formal, i.e. the mode of production itself had as yet no specifically capitalist character."[15] As we will see, workers wanted to escape from these relations; this put the reproduction of wage labor in question. However, as capital came up against barriers to its growth, it proceeded over time to *alter* the mode of production it inherited and change it into one that corresponded to its needs and requirements. With the development of manufacturing and, then, capital's factory system, a specifically capitalist mode of production emerged in which workers were *really* subsumed under capital within production.

As noted in earlier chapters, these changes played an absolutely critical role in the completion of capitalism as an organic system. Not only was a reserve army of labor constantly replenished, but the development of capitalist production increasingly generated the appearance that machinery (and fixed capital in general) was the embodiment and source of all productivity and wealth. Thus both the dependence and feeling of dependence of workers upon capital were regularly reproduced; that is, capital's requirements increasingly appeared as "self-evident natural laws." As Marx declared, "The organization of the capitalist process of production, once it is fully developed, breaks down all resistance." With the development of the specifically capitalist mode of production, capital could now produce its most critical premise, the working class it needs: "The silent compulsion of economic relations sets the seal on the domination of the capitalist over the worker."[16]

Thus, for Marx, the development of the specifically capitalist mode of production marked capitalism's success "in subordinating all elements of society to itself or creating out of it the organs which it still lacks." But what ensures the reproduction of the worker as wage laborer *before* capital has "posited the mode of production corresponding to it"?[17]

The Capitalist Mode of Regulation

"Centuries are required," Marx commented, "before the 'free' worker, owing to the greater development of the capitalist mode of production, makes a voluntary agreement, that is, is compelled by social conditions to sell the whole of his active life, his very capacity for labour, in return for the price of his customary means of subsistence, to sell his birth-right for a mess of pottage."[18] Until the development of the specifically capitalist mode of production, workers did *not* look upon the requirements of capitalist production as self-evident but, rather, "by education, tradition, and habit" considered the sale of their labor power as unnatural.[19]

What, though, was the alternative for workers? To produce for themselves—in short, *not* to sell their labor power to the capitalist. Where it was possible, workers extracted themselves from wage labor. If wages rose, for example, they could meet their monetary requirements and spend more time on other activity—and this was especially true for those engaged in handicraft activity or who combined handicraft work for wages with cultivation of the soil. And wages *did* tend to rise with the growth of capital based upon the inherited mode of production—given the labor-intensive nature of production, "the demand for wage-labour therefore grew rapidly with every accumulation of capital, while the supply only followed slowly behind."[20] The implication was a tendency for the non-reproduction of wage labor.

Increased wages under these conditions also provided an opportunity for workers to *save* in order to extract themselves from wage labor, and this opportunity was especially marked in the colonies of the New World. There, Marx noted, "today's wage-labourer is tomorrow's independent peasant or artisan,

working for himself"; in the colonies, there is "a constant transformation of wage-labourers into independent producers." The
result? "Not only does the degree of exploitation of the wage-
labourer remain indecently low . . . [but] the wage labourer also
loses, along with the relation of dependence, the feeling of
dependence on the abstemious capitalist."[21]

In short, in the colonies the relative supply and demand for
workers meant that the relationship of wage labor was not being
reproduced: where "the worker receives more than is required for
the reproduction of his labour capacity and very soon becomes a
peasant farming independently, etc., the original relation is not
constantly reproduced."[22] And that meant that the reproduction
of capital was threatened because the reproduction of the worker
as wage laborer "is the absolutely necessary condition for capitalist production."[23] In the absence of the specifically capitalist
mode of production, rising wages tended both to slow down the
expanded reproduction of capital and to encourage the non-
reproduction of wage labor.[24]

"Two diametrically opposed economic systems" were in
struggle in the colonies—one based upon capitalist relations and
the other where the producer "as owner of his own conditions of
labour, employs that labour to enrich himself instead of the capitalist."[25] That struggle, however, was not limited to the New
World. Indeed, the development of capitalism in the Old World
was a process in which "the free proprietor of the conditions of
his labour" was "supplanted by capitalist private property, which
rests on the exploitation of alien, but formally free labour."[26]

"Becoming" has two sides—an "arising" and also a "pass-
ing-away." In primitive capitalist accumulation, the means of
production and labor power, the essential elements of the capitalist labor process, are *extracted from somewhere else*. The other
side of the subsuming of producers, means of production, and
the labor process itself under capitalist relations, accordingly,
was their detachment from preexisting relations. In short, the

process of becoming of capitalist relations involved the *con-tracted* reproduction of those existing relations within which production hitherto had taken place. Thus there is a *contested* reproduction, a process in which differing relations exist simul-taneously and there is a struggle over the subordination of the elements of production.

Contested reproduction, though, did not end with the origi-nal (or primitive) development of capitalist relations of produc-tion. Expanded reproduction of those new relations was not secure until the development of a specific mode of production that ensures reproduction of the premises of the system: "As soon as capitalist production stands on its own feet, it not only main-tains this separation [between workers and the means of produc-tion] but reproduces it on a constantly extending scale."[27] Until capital has developed upon its foundations, those "two diametri-cally opposed economic systems" coexist.

This point is essential to recognize because, as the Soviet economist Evgeny Preobrazhensky pointed out in the 1920s, two systems and two logics do not simply exist side by side. They *interact*. They interpenetrate. They *deform* each other. Precisely because there is contested reproduction between differing sets of productive relations, the interaction of the systems can generate crises, inefficiencies, and irrationality that wouldn't be found in either system in its purity.[28] And this was exactly what was occur-ring when the accumulation of capital produced the tendency described above for the non-reproduction of wage labor as the result of rising wages.

How, then, were capitalist relations of production reproduced under these conditions? Marx was quite clear on what occurred. He detailed the measures undertaken with the emergence of cap-italism in the Old World—"the bloody discipline," the "police methods," "the state compulsion to confine the struggle between capital and labour within limits convenient for capital." In direct contrast to the conditions for the reproduction of capitalist relations once the specifically capitalist mode of production has been developed, "the rising bourgeoisie needs the power of the state, and uses it to 'regulate' wages."[29]

As I argued in "The Socialist Fetter Considered," Marx's view was that until capital produced its own premises, it "needed a particular 'mode of regulation' (defined as 'institutional forms, procedures and habits which either coerce or persuade private agents to conform to its schemas'). That specific mode of regulation relied upon the coercive power of the state to ensure the compatibility of the behaviour of workers with the requirements of capital."[30] In the absence of "the sheer force of economic relations," capital used the state to prevent wages from rising and to compel workers (through "grotesquely terroristic laws") "into accepting the discipline necessary for the system of wage-labour."[31]

Capital similarly drew upon state power to ensure reproduction of capitalist productive relations in the North American settlements, where workers could save to escape wage labor. In order to prevent the restoration of the private property of workers in their means of production (and the reproduction of forms of production resting upon the personal labor of the independent producer), capital found its answer in specific state regulations:

> In the old civilized countries the worker, although free, is by a law of nature dependent on the capitalist; in colonies this dependence must be created by artificial means.[32]

That was the "secret" discovered in the New World by the political economy of the Old World: *The conditions necessary for the reproduction of a set of productive relations differ according to whether there is in existence an organic system or whether that system is in the state of becoming.*[33]

Alternative Paths?

If a capitalist mode of regulation is required before capitalism has developed upon its own foundations, nothing requires it (or, indeed, the rupture of property rights or the seizure of production) to be identical in all countries where capitalism emerges. In discussing the process of "becoming" sketched out in *Capital*, we are not considering a logical process but rather a specific historical path. Insofar as new relations of production "do not develop out of nothing, nor drop from the sky, nor from the womb of the self-positing Idea; but from within and in antithesis to the existing development of production and the inherited, traditional relations of production," the possibility of alternative paths is obvious.[34]

Marx was absolutely clear that the original (or primitive) accumulation of the elements that form capitalist relations of production did *not* have to follow the classic form it took in England. Although it is the basis of the process, he wrote in his initial editions of *Capital*, the expropriation of the peasant "in different countries, assumes different aspects, and runs through its various phases in different orders of succession, and at different periods." That recognition of the possibility of alternative paths became stronger in the French edition, in which Marx explicitly limited the account in *Capital* to "all the other countries of Western Europe." He reinforced this point a few years later in a letter, insisting that "the chapter on primitive accumulation claims no more than to trace the path by which, in Western Europe, the capitalist economic order emerged from the womb of the feudal economic order."

Do not transform "my historical sketch of the genesis of capitalism in Western Europe into a historico-philosophical theory of the general course fatally imposed on all peoples, whatever the historical circumstances in which they find themselves placed," Marx demanded.[35] Indeed, Marx became increasingly conscious of historical contingency in his later years as he closely studied

communal land ownership in Russia and elsewhere. In his ethno-
logical notebooks, he noted that it was wrong to describe "the
dissolution of communal ownership of land in Punjab as if it took
place as an inevitable consequence of the *economic progress* in
spite of the affectionate attitude of the British toward this archaic
form. The truth is rather that the British themselves are the *principal* (and active) *offenders* responsible for this dissolution."
Similarly, in his draft letters to Vera Zasulich, he stressed that
"what threatens the life of the Russian commune is neither a historical inevitability nor a theory; it is state oppression, and
exploitation by capitalist intruders whom the state has made powerful at the peasants' expense."[36]

Yet Marx was not questioning what was necessary for capitalism to emerge—only the insistence that it had to happen in a *particular* way. Certainly he did not waver from the view that the
expropriation of peasants (in the Russian case from their communal property) remained the condition for transforming them into
the wage laborers needed for capitalist relations of production.
Indeed, it was not necessary to drive them from the land as in
England or by a decree abolishing communal property from
above; high tax demands imposed upon peasants could be sufficient to lead them to abandon the land.[37] In short, *some* process
by which existing property rights were ruptured remained necessary to create the historical premise of capital, on the one hand,
and wage labor on the other.

Certainly we may note that the assembly of elements characteristic of capitalist relations and mode of regulation assumed different aspects in different countries. In Japan, for example, the
state did far more than function as a mode of regulation for the
maintenance of capitalist relations of production; it played a critical role in the initial creation of the conditions for the development of capitalism by capturing the feudal rents from the land
(paying for this in the form of bonds) and using this income to
create new means of production in modern industry, railways,

and shipping that were subsequently sold to the emerging capitalist class. The state-directed abolition of serfdom in Prussia and
Russia, as well as the creation by the state in Germany and France
of major financial vehicles whereby the substantial wealth of large
landowners could be directed to the creation of new capitalist
enterprises, were all variations on the classic account that Marx
provided in *Capital*. All were part of the process of the emergence
of capitalism, and the specific characteristics of those national
capitalisms would reflect the way in which capitalist relations of
production emerged and were sustained by the state "in antithesis to the existing development of production and the inherited,
traditional relations of production."

But what if capital had *not* been able to use the state to ensure
the conditions of its expanded reproduction? In fact, every step
of the process before the development of the new mode of production is one which, to a greater or lesser degree, contains
within it the opposite possibility—that is, the reversal of that
process. And the crises and irrationalities that are the product of
contested reproduction bring the barriers facing the emerging
system to the surface. If there is *neither* the specifically capitalist
mode of production *nor* a mode of regulation that ensures the
reproduction of wage laborers who are dependent upon capital,
then, as Marx revealed in his discussion of the colonies, capitalism is not irreversible. The path, in fact, can lead backward.

This point is precisely what we need to keep in mind when
considering the becoming of *socialism*—the necessity for a socialist mode of regulation that can ensure the reproduction of socialist relations until such time that socialism has succeeded in developing all the organs it requires as an organic system.

5. The Concept of a Socialist Transition

What is socialism? For many people schooled in the texts of the twentieth century, the following propositions essentially hold:

1. Socialism involves the replacement of the private ownership of the means of production by state ownership.
2. Socialism is the first stage after capitalism and is succeeded by the higher stage, communism.
3. Development of the productive forces is the condition for communism.
4. The principle of distribution appropriate to socialism and the development of productive forces is in accordance with one's contribution.

In short, socialism in this received doctrine is the stage in which you develop productive forces and thereby prepare the way for the higher stage. Further, an important characteristic of the socialist stage is the place of material incentive, the application of the "socialist principle" of "from each according to his ability, to each according to his work."

The Soviet Constitution of 1936 offers a classic version of this vision of socialism. According to Article 11, socialism is a society in which economic life is "determined and directed by the state national economic plan with the aim of increasing the public wealth, of steadily improving the material conditions of the working people and raising their cultural level." Article 12 reads that "In the U.S.S.R. work is a duty and a matter of honor for every able-bodied citizen, in accordance with the principle: 'He who does not work, neither shall he eat.' The principle applied in the U.S.S.R. is that of socialism: 'From each according to his ability, to each according to his work.'"[1]

Where did this concept of two stages and a specific "socialist principle" come from? The immediate source was Lenin. Reading Marx's distinction in his *Critique of the Gotha Programme* between the new society as it initially emerges and the society once it has produced its own foundations, Lenin labeled these as two separate stages, socialism and communism. He asked in *State and Revolution*, what would be the character of the state after capitalism? His answer was that it varied: a state would be unnecessary in the higher stage of communism. However, a state would clearly be required within socialism. Why? *Because until such time as it was possible to distribute products in accordance with needs and until such time as it was possible to allow people to choose whatever activities they wished, a state was necessary.*

The state was necessary within this lower stage of socialism, Lenin argued, in order to apply the rule of law as "regulator (determining factor) in the distribution of products and the allotment of labour among the members of society." Indeed, he insisted, *until the higher stage*, "the *strictest* control by society *and by the state* over the measure of labour and the measure of consumption" would be essential. He who does not work shall not eat was one principle that would be applied strictly—as would "the other socialist principle, 'An equal amount of products for an equal amount of labour.'"[2]

Further, this need for the state to regulate "the quantity of products to be received by each" would continue until the socialist stage brought about "an enormous development of productive forces." The latter would be the "economic basis for the complete withering away of the state" and the development of communism. "To each according to his needs" would be possible as a basis of distribution for people only "when their labour becomes so productive that they will voluntarily work *according to their ability*."[3]

But was this conception of two stages—"stages of economic ripeness"—and of the specific socialist principle consistent with Marx's view? In his *Critique of the Gotha Programme*, Marx did indeed distinguish between a communist society "as it has *developed* on its own foundations" and one "just as it *emerges* from capitalist society; which is thus in every respect, economically, morally and intellectually, still stamped with the birthmarks of the old society from whose womb it emerges." Further, he explicitly recognized that it was "inevitable" that the latter society "when it has just emerged after prolonged birth pangs from capitalist society" would be characterized by "defects"—defects such as the orientation toward an exchange of equivalents (where "the same amount of labour which he has given to society in one form he receives back in another form").

However, this conception of two separate stages distorts Marx's perspective. Marx described a *single organic system*—a system that necessarily emerges initially from capitalism with *defects*. Like every organic system, that system is in the process of *becoming*; it is a system that begins not with premises that it itself has produced but rather with *historical* premises, *inherited* elements. Accordingly, like other organic systems in the process of becoming, like capitalism itself, socialism must go beyond what it has inherited to produce its *own* premises; it has to generate premises in their *socialist* economic form.

Once socialism does produce its own premises, then we can say that the system "has *developed* on its own foundations." This process of development is the process of becoming the organic system of socialism: "*Its development to a totality consists precisely in subordinating all elements of society to itself, or in creating out of it the organs it still lacks.* This is historically how it becomes a totality."[4]

All this should be quite familiar after the last chapter. As I commented there:

> We will never understand Marx's conception of socialism or what he had to say about economic systems if we don't grasp the essential distinction between the "becoming" of a system and its "being"—that is, the distinction between the historical emergence of a particular form of society and the nature of that society *once it has developed upon its own foundations.*

Why should we accept that Marx abandoned his dialectical understanding of the Being and Becoming of an organic system and substituted for it a concept of discrete stages with differing principles?

Indeed, it is by means of the designation of separate stages of socialism and communism that an alien principle has been smuggled into a Marxist conception of socialism. Recall our discussion in chapter 3 on the "solidarian society." Marx understood that the exchange relation of an equal amount of products for an equal amount of labor is a defect that must be *struggled* against, a "right of inequality" that views members of this society "*only as workers* and nothing more is seen in them, everything else being ignored." This one-sided conception, Marx recognized, does not look upon producers as human beings. It stands in contrast to a *different* relation—what a person is entitled to "in his capacity as a member of society."[5]

In short, a defect that must be *subordinated* if socialism is to develop was transformed by the received doctrine into *a princi-*

ple that must be enforced by the state! But how do you build the new society based upon a defect?[6] How do you build the new society by relying upon self-interest and the desire of owners of labor power for an equivalent return for their activity?

As Che knew (and as the twentieth century demonstrated), reliance upon "individual material interest as the lever" is a "pipe dream." However, that reliance upon "the dull instruments left to us by capitalism" does more than merely "lead into a blind alley." To build upon material self-interest is to build upon an element from the *old society*; and, as we have seen, it tends to undermine both social ownership and social production organized by workers. Very simply, *material self-interest points backward*! It points back toward capitalism.

NAMING THE SYSTEM

So let us forget about this concept of a specific "socialist principle" based upon material self-interest. And let us replace this received doctrine of two distinct stages with Marx's idea of a single organic system in the process of becoming. But, if there is only one system, what should we *name* it? Socialism, communism . . . or something else? Marx generally called it communism—especially in his mature work, and I have followed Marx in this respect in the past.[7] However, I no longer think this is the appropriate terminology to use in the twenty-first century.

The term *communism* communicated something different when Marx wrote in the nineteenth century. Communism was the name Marx used to describe the society of free and associated producers—"an association of free men, working with the means of production held in common, and expending their many different forms of labour-power in full self-awareness as one single social labour force."[8] *But very few people think of communism that way now.* In fact, people hardly think of communism as an economic system, as a way in which producers organize to produce for the needs of all! Rather, as the result of the understanding of the experiences of the last century, communism is now viewed as a *political* system—in particular, *as a state that stands over and above society and oppresses working people.*

Can we ignore the way in which the experience of the twentieth century has grasped the minds of the people who must be reached? Concepts and names matter. In *State and Revolution*, Lenin called attention to Engels's refusal to use the term "Social-Democrat" because "at that time the Proudhonists in France and the Lassalleans in Germany called themselves Social-Democrats."[9] It was a political decision under concrete circumstances. The same logic applies, I think, to anyone at this time more interested in transforming society than in scholasticism.

As indicated in the Introduction to this book, we have to "reinvent" socialism. That is another reason to stress the term that the Young Marx employed when describing "the goal of human development, the form of human society"—*socialism.* Human society, true social life, humanism, socialism—all conveyed for Marx the vision of a society in which the alienation of human beings from their activity, their lives, other human beings and nature has come to an end. A society where our productive activity affirms our human nature, socialism—"the unity of man with man, which is based on the real differences between men"—was Marx's goal. It must be ours. [10]

THE BECOMING OF SOCIALISM:
THE RUPTURE

But how does this new system *become*? Firstly, we need to begin from the recognition that what drives socialism forward is "the worker's own need for development." Whereas the impulse for the development of capitalism comes from capital's "ought" (its drive for surplus value) and whereas capitalism develops by going beyond the barriers to capital's growth, in the same way, socialism develops by going beyond the barriers to the workers' "ought," the drive of workers for their own development.[11]

We see, in short, that in their struggle to get beyond these barriers, workers transform both circumstances and themselves. This is a process of substituting for the logic of capital the logic of human development. And in this process the dynamics of capitalism, its laws of motion, are superseded by laws of motion of the society of associated producers:

> The present "spontaneous action of the natural laws of capital and landed property" can only be superseded by "the spontaneous action of the laws of the social economy of free and associated labour" in a long process of development of new conditions, as was the "spontaneous action of the economic laws of slavery" and the "spontaneous action of the economic laws of serfdom."[12]

Consider the classic picture that Marx offered for the becoming of socialism. Its sequence begins with the emergence of a specific social relationship among workers—relations subordinate to the dominant capital/wage-labor relation but developing in the course of their struggles against capital. Beginning by attempting to end the competition among themselves as sellers of labor power, workers organize in trade unions to prevent wages from being driven downward. As they are brought together by capital in the process of production, their degree of separation falls, and with it "so too their resistance to the domination of capital" increases. They come to recognize their unity in the course of struggle against capital. Yet capital's power is not simply the power of individual capitalists against groups of employees; rather, capital's power as the owner of the products of social labor is its ultimate power, and that is the power of capital as a whole.[13]

The growing recognition that "in its merely economic action capital is the stronger side" accordingly propels workers into political action. They come to recognize the necessity to struggle as a class politically—through a "political movement, that is to say, a movement of the class, with the object of enforcing its interests in a general form, in a form possessing general, socially coercive force." This was, Marx stressed, the message of the International Working Men's Association: "To conquer political power has therefore become the great duty of the working classes."[14] And it was the message that Marx and Engels continued to stress in the *Communist Manifesto*: "The first step in the revolution by the working class is to raise the proletariat to the position of ruling class, to win the battle of democracy."

In that scenario, workers struggle to win that "battle of democracy" and to use their control of the state to remove the economic basis for capitalism and a class society. With its successful conquest of political power, Marx and Engels predicted, "the proletariat will use its political supremacy to wrest, by degrees, all capital from the bourgeoisie, to centralise all instruments of production in the hands of the State, i.e., of the proletariat organized as the ruling class; and to increase the total of productive forces as rapidly as possible."[15] "By *degrees*": the *Communist Manifesto* envisioned a process of "despotic inroads" upon capital—a process in which the reproduction of capital is constrained, and the proletariat finds itself always compelled to move forward. In place of the monopolization of the means of production by the capitalist class, there increasingly emerges common ownership of the means of production.

Thus the rupture of property rights. But another rupture, too. Because the scenario essentially breaks off here, and aside from scattered observations and insights (such as those produced by the Paris Commune), what remains are those bare outlines of the process of becoming that Marx introduced in his *Critique of the Gotha Programme*. To say anything more requires a rational reconstruction of the process of becoming based upon the elements we have before us. Where there are missing pieces, we have to try to infer them by posing a question as to the probability of the known in the absence of the existence of specific unknowns.

WHAT IS TO BE SUBORDINATED

To explore theoretically the process of the becoming of socialism, it is important to begin with the concept of socialism as an organic system—in other words, to let theory guide our understanding of the process of becoming. That concept, we have seen, incorporates three moments: (1) the social ownership of the means of production (which includes the right of all to share in our social heritage); (2) social production organized by workers (which allows producers to develop all their capacities through their practice); and (3) satisfaction of communal needs and purposes (which requires development of a solidarian society based upon recognition of our common humanity).

We begin precisely from that "association of free men, working with the means of production held in common, and expending their many different forms of labour-power in full self-awareness as one single social labour force." With that vision clearly in mind, we are able to identify exactly what elements of the old society must be subordinated: (a) the private ownership of the means of production, (b) the despotism of the workplace and (c) production for self-interest.

But how? Let us recall the moments in Marx's story of the becoming of capitalism. We begin with an existing but subordinated social relation: the orientation of merchant and money-lending capital toward the expansion of value. A key point occurs with the rupture of property rights that is a necessary condition for new productive relations. However, that change is in itself insufficient—the new actors must "seize possession of production" for the emergence of this new relation of production. Those relations of production in turn remain unstable until the development of a specific mode of production that supports their reproduction—that, in short, produces as its result the premises of the system. Is this a useful template for exploring the becoming of socialism?

Come back to the point of that critical rupture in property rights. Is the change in ownership that makes the means of production state property sufficient to create relations of production organized by the associated producers? *No more than the earlier rupture of property rights was sufficient in itself for the emergence of capitalist relations of production.* In order to establish the "system of the association of free and equal producers," the producers themselves must "seize possession of production" and introduce cooperative production based upon common ownership of the means of production. What, though, is the probability of this occurring unless the associated producers seize possession of the *state*?[16]

The capitalist state, as Marx understood, was *infected*—its very institutions involve a "systematic and hierarchic division of labour," and it assumes the character of a public force organized for social enslavement, of an engine of class despotism.[17] That is why Marx and Engels concluded that the working class "cannot simply lay hold of the ready-made state machinery, and use it for its own purpose."[18] How can the means of production be possessed by the associated producers when they are owned by a state whose very nature is hierarchy and power over all from above?

The recognition that workers could not use the existing capitalist state for their own purposes, though, was not Marx's discovery. Rather, it was the spontaneous discovery of workers in the Paris Commune. There was the demonstration that a workers' state is one in which public functions become the functions of workers "instead of the hidden attributes of a trained caste"; it was the discovery in practice that workers need a *new* state, one that is democratic and decentralized. *At last*, Marx proclaimed, the necessary form of the workers' state has been discovered: the Commune was "the political form at last discovered under which to work out the economical emancipation of Labour." Here was the state that would "serve as a lever for uprooting the economical foundations upon which rests the existence of classes, and therefore of class-rule."[19]

"All France," Marx commented about the general direction of the Commune, "would have been organized into self-working and self-governing communes." The Commune pointed to the destruction of state power insofar as that state stood above society—"its legitimate functions were to be wrested from an authority usurping pre-eminence over society itself, and restored to the responsible agents of society." It was "the reabsorption of the state power by society as its own living forces instead of as forces controlling and subduing it, by the popular masses themselves, forming their own force instead of the organised force of their suppression—the political form of their social emancipation."[20]

Characteristic of this particular form of rule "at last discovered" was the "self-government of the producers," and that meant at every level of society. "The thing," Marx pointed out, "starts with self-government of the township."[21] The implications are clear: with the conversion of the state "from an organ superimposed upon society into one completely subordinate to it," self-governing producers can wield the state for their own purposes, continuously changing both circumstances and themselves.[22] What we see, in short, is the development of yet another aspect of the social relationship of producers—they are linked as self-governing citizens in the project of acting in the interests of producers as a whole.

But is such a new state consistent with despotism in the workplace? On the contrary, it should be self-evident that such a state requires that the associated producers are the possessors of production, that its condition of existence is that that there are socialist relations of production. Self-governing producers, self-managing citizens—they form part of a coherent whole; and the process of their development is the subordination of the inheritance from the old society—the "systematic and hierarchic division of labour," the "engine of class despotism" characteristic of both the capitalist workplace and the capitalist state.

How probable, on the other hand, is it that the old hierarchical state will tend to foster the organization of production by workers, that process necessary to permit the full development of their capacities, both individual and collective? Far more likely that the spontaneous tendency of such a state, "the organised force" of the suppression of the popular masses, will be to reproduce

> the delusion as if administration and political governing were
> mysteries, transcendent functions only to be trusted to the hands
> of a trained caste—state parasites, richly paid sycophants and
> sinecurists, in the higher posts, absorbing the intelligence of the
> masses and turning them against themselves in the lower places
> of the hierarchy.[23]

In this respect, the struggle for the new socialist relations of production is a struggle on *two* fronts—within the workplace and within the state that is the owner of the means of production. To the extent that struggle is successful, we can speak of the emergence of "the cooperative society based upon common ownership of the means of production." And now, the very methods and organization of production can be changed. Within socialist relations of production, the associated producers can begin to change the mode of production they inherited and create a mode of production that corresponds to *their* needs and goals—in short, a specifically socialist mode of production.

Obviously, we cannot know in advance the precise characteristics of the socialist mode of production as they will be developed by the associated producers themselves. However, one point can be predicted with reasonable certainty—*that new mode of production will not correspond to the capitalist mode of production*. After all, the specifically capitalist mode of production was developed as capital proceeded to subordinate all elements of society *to itself* and to create the organs *it* still lacked. This was "the historical reshaping of the traditional, inherited means of labour into a form adequate to capital."[24] The productive forces developed under capitalism flow from and reflect the particular set of relations of production characteristic of capitalism.

Accordingly, it is essential to recognize that *those new productive forces were not neutral*. "Peculiar to and characteristic" of the productive forces that capital develops is that "they distort the worker into a fragment of a man, they degrade him to the level of an appendage of a machine, they destroy the actual content of his labour by turning it into a torment; they alienate from him the intellectual potentialities of the labour process . . . ; they deform the conditions under which he works." Indeed, "within the capitalist system," Marx commented, "all methods for raising the social productivity of labour are put into effect at the cost of the individual worker."[25]

All new productive forces aren't like that. After all, what is the probability that associated producers who possess the process of production would introduce productive forces that cripple them? On the contrary, we would expect that the specific productive forces developed by associated producers would be characterized by that "inverse situation in which objective wealth is there to satisfy the worker's own need for development." Rather than dividing, crippling, or otherwise harming producers, we may predict that the productive forces introduced by associated producers will be oriented toward the development of rich human beings.

The development of productive forces is thus not an abstraction. If we learn anything from volume 1 of Marx's *Capital*, it is

that what matters are *particular* productive forces. Capital introduced specific alterations in the mode of production in order to
achieve its class goals. In the same way, socialism, that society of
associated producers, can only develop as the associated producers alter the mode of production in such a way as to realize
their goals.

Of course, the new socialist mode of production developed
within socialist relations of production would not be put into
place overnight. As in the case of the development of the specifically capitalist mode of production, the process of becoming of
the new mode of production is likely to occur as the associated
producers come up against barriers to the realization of their
goals and therefore proceed to transcend the existing structures.
As the ways in which we produce become processes of conscious cooperation oriented toward satisfying the needs of all
within the community, monopolization of our social heritage,
domination from above within our productive activity and lives,
and producing for our self-interest increasingly would be understood to be irrational and atavistic. In this way, the productive
forces generated under socialist relations would develop a body
of associated producers that "by education, tradition and habit
looks upon the requirements of that mode of production as self-
evident natural laws."[26]

This socialist mode of production, in short, would tend to
spontaneously produce a new common sense, one that looks upon
social ownership, social production organized by workers and
production for social needs as self-evidently rational. Just as the
development of the specifically capitalist mode of production is an
essential part of the reproduction of the worker as wage laborer
within capitalism, so too would the socialist mode of production
create the producers the new society needs. But what happens in
the *absence* of the specifically socialist mode of production?

THE SOCIALIST MODE OF REGULATION

How does the new socialist system become an organic system by subordinating the defects it has inherited? How does it ensure the reproduction of socialist relations of production? In the same way capitalism did. Until such time that a new socialist mode of production has been constructed, *a socialist mode of regulation is required*. As in the case of the becoming of capitalism, "the power of the state" is needed. But not the power of a hierarchical state organized as an "engine of class despotism." That cannot be the political form for the social emancipation of workers.

On the contrary, "whereas capitalism, which needs for its reproduction the acquiescence of workers, can draw upon the coercive power of the state for this purpose, such a resort is entirely alien to the co-operative society based on common ownership of the means of production."[27] Indeed, "how could such a self-managing and self-governing society emerge on the basis of a mode of regulation in which producers are coerced into suppressing behaviour which to them appears as natural and self-evidently rational?" Rather than producing people fit to found society anew, coercion from above merely produces "private, atomized individuals who endure until what is unnatural is removed."

Here is the critical question—"what mode of regulation is appropriate for socialism insofar as its requirements do not appear as self-evident natural laws?"[28] As Marx grasped, an essential part of the socialist mode of regulation is the power of decentralized, democratic, "self-working and self-governing communes"—a state of the Paris Commune type. Just as capitalism required force—"the midwife of every old society which is pregnant with a new one"—so too does the emerging socialist society require force appropriate to the new society.

Through its own specific "artificial means," the socialist mode of regulation attempts to foster the new relations that are developing among the associated producers. Inherited elements such as the emphasis upon individual self-interest are subordinated by developing *a new social rationality*—one that focuses upon the community and its needs and encourages the development of new social norms based upon cooperation and solidarity among members of society. The combination of that focus and the creation of communal institutions that democratically identify communal needs and coordinate productive activity to satisfy those needs is at the center of the new socialist common sense.

As I stressed in "The Socialist Fetter: A Cautionary Tale":

> More than simply focus on the centrality of human needs, however, what is critical is that the necessity to engage in collective solutions to their satisfaction becomes recognised as a responsibility of all individuals. Where a sense of community and a confidence in the benefits of acting "in full self-awareness as a single social labour force" are called for, a state over and above civil society cannot produce the people who have these characteristics. Rather, only through their own activities through autonomous organisations—at the neighbourhood, community and national levels—can people transform both circumstances and themselves. What is called for, in short, is the conscious development of a socialist civil society.[29]

This concept of the socialist mode of regulation rests upon the principle that Che understood—that to build socialism, "it is necessary, simultaneous with the new material foundations, to build the new man."[30] Until such time as the associated producers develop new productive forces that are appropriate to and spontaneously support the relations of production of associated producers, consciously fostering this set of institutional arrangements and ideological campaigns is essential to support the reproduction of the new productive relations. For how long? Clearly, the necessity for such a mode of regulation would differ in different societies; as in the case of capitalism, we can anticipate that there would be variations reflecting "the existing development of production and the inherited, traditional relations of production."

CONTESTED REPRODUCTION

Nevertheless, even with a socialist mode of regulation, the reproduction of socialism will always be contingent until the development of a specifically socialist mode of production. Indeed, in the absence of *both* the specifically socialist mode of production and an effective socialist mode of regulation, socialism is not irreversible.

Hugo Chávez has often quoted Gramsci's statement about an interregnum in which the old is dying but the new cannot yet be born. The image is powerful. But it is misleading. In fact, the old is *not* dying—it is always struggling to survive and to renew itself. And the new may *already have been born*—but it is always in a struggle to survive.

After all, even if private ownership of the means of production has been ended, the continued presence of hierarchy in the workplace and self-interest as a motivating force in production are elements of the old society that threaten to subordinate the new. As we have seen in chapters 2 and 3, the tendency of these old elements is to dissolve the socialist triangle. On the other hand, inroads made by the invading socialist society, such as the introduction of democratic decision making in the workplace and the community and the focus upon production for communal needs and purposes, point in the opposite direction—toward the *completion* of the socialist triangle. Characteristic of contested reproduction is the coexistence of both tendencies.

Significantly, when Chávez quotes Gramsci, he has left out a rather important part of Gramsci's observation: in this interregnum, "a great many morbid symptoms appear." In this interregnum, both the old and new exist side by side. And the implication? We should remember Preobrazhensky's insight (noted in chapter 4) that when you have two different systems side by side, you can get the worst of both worlds. Precisely because there are two coexisting and interpenetrating systems, that combination can produce system irrationality.

For example, when producers function as private owners of labor power and attempt to maximize what they obtain for every expenditure of their labor, then the development of production for communal needs will clearly affect their incentive to provide labor in their exchange with society. (Why should they work if they can get what they need *without* this exchange?) Looked at from the other angle, the continuation of alienated production (because of the character of the workplace and the focus upon self-interest) will ensure that workers do not develop their capacities but that their need to consume alien products continues to grow. From both perspectives, this combination is incoherent.

The logic of the old system weighs like a nightmare on the brains of the living. At every moment of crisis or the momentary failure of goals, there will be some who will declare that "the people are not ready" and that, accordingly, it is necessary to rely upon what they *are* ready for ("one-man management," material incentives, private ownership and entrepreneurship and the like). Citing Marx's *Gotha Critique* statement that "right can never be higher than the economic structure of society and its cultural development conditioned thereby," they argue that only after the sufficient development of the productive forces "can the narrow horizon of bourgeois right be fully left behind." The old story—everything depends upon the development of the productive forces.

Any productive forces? And created and nurtured within *any* relations of production? How that horizon of bourgeois right will ever be surpassed with productive forces developed outside socialist relations and with the constant generation of new, alienated needs is never explained.[31] Genuflection to the abstract concept of the development of productive forces is the way in which attention is diverted from what Marx knew was essential—the nature of productive relations.

In this interregnum, two paths emerge. Each emanates from a particular perspective. Each identifies different defects. From the perspective of capitalism, the irrationalities and inefficiencies are the result of socialist elements. From the perspective of socialism, on the other hand, the irrationalities and inefficiencies are the result of the continued presence of the elements inherited from capitalism. Two paths—one going back toward capitalism and one advancing toward socialism. We come, then, to Lenin's famous question, "Who will win?" There is nothing inevitable about the answer.

THE CONCEPT OF A SOCIALIST TRANSITION

Consider the propositions with which we began this chapter:

1. Socialism involves the replacement of the private ownership of the means of production by state ownership.
2. Socialism is the first stage after capitalism and is succeeded by the higher stage, communism.
3. Development of the productive forces is the condition for communism.
4. The principle of distribution appropriate to socialism and the development of productive forces is in accordance with one's contribution.

On the basis of the discussion in this chapter, it is appropriate to substitute alternative propositions:

1. Socialism, the cooperative society based upon common ownership of the means of production, has as its premise

that the associated producers possess the process of production (that is, socialist relations of production).

2. This new system inevitably emerges with defects it inherits from capitalism. Its development into an organic system "consists precisely in subordinating all elements of society to itself, or in creating out of it the organs which it still lacks."

3. The emergence of socialism as an organic system that produces its own premises and thereby develops on its own foundations depends upon the creation of a specifically socialist mode of production; until that is in place, the reproduction of socialist relations of production requires the existence of a socialist mode of regulation.

4. An essential part of the development of this socialist mode of regulation is the substitution for the self-orientation characteristic of owners of labor power (with its insistence upon equivalents), the principle in which people are *not* regarded *"only as workers"* (with "everything else being ignored") but rather as members of society. The new principle socialism introduces, "the socialist principle," expands *"that which is intended for the common satisfaction of needs* . . . in proportion as the new society develops."[32] It thus fosters a new relation, a communal society in which productive activity is undertaken not out of self-interest but where communal needs and purposes are understood as the basis of our activity.

In the two chapters that follow, we will attempt to explore these questions concretely.

6. Making a Path to Socialism

If you don't know where you want to go, no road will take you there. However, knowing *where* you want to go is only the first part; it's not at all the same as knowing *how* to get there.

Every path is different. We all have different starting points. We live in countries with different levels of economic development, economic structures (the weight that agriculture has, for example), and balance of political forces. We have different experiences and capacities born from struggles and different traditions, culture, and constraints inherent in our particular geographies and environment. This means that the paths we take toward the common goal of the full development of human potential will be different. Some paths indeed will be longer than others. Further, given the complex of different obstacles we face, some paths to socialism for the twenty-first century will be relatively straight, while others will require many switchbacks.

Obviously, we can't proceed as if there is a single path to socialism. "The categorical requirement of Marxist theory in investigating any social question," Lenin understood, "is that it be examined within *definite* historical limits, and, if it refers to a particular country (e.g., the national programme for a given country), that account be taken of the specific features distinguishing that country from others in the same historical epoch." [1]

Isn't there, then, a significant danger of positing a universal "transitional program" independent of particular concrete circumstances? We may agree that there are necessary presuppositions of socialism—social ownership of the means of production, worker management of production, and a solidarian society in which we produce for the purpose of communal needs; however, *the way* in which these are to be achieved is not dictated. We have to remember Marx's own understanding of the importance of contingency. If we insist upon a single program, we lapse into "a historico-philosophical theory of the general course fatally imposed on all peoples, whatever the historical circumstances in which they find themselves placed." In short, it is essential to recognize that every country must invent its *own* path,

Is there, for example, a necessary order to the steps along the path to socialism? Must the historical order follow the logical order traced in preceding chapters—(1) social ownership of the means of production, (2) worker management and, finally, (3) a solidarian society? If we insist upon this historical sequence, we are forgetting an essential point—the *interdependence* of the three sides of the socialist triangle. "How, indeed, could the single logical formula of movement, of sequence, of time, explain the structure of society in which all relations coexist simultaneously and support one another?" [2]

After all, capitalism is clearly a structure in which all relations support one another. That old society cannot disappear overnight. For example, every moment that people act within old relations is a process of reproducing old ideas and attitudes. Working within a hierarchy, functioning without the ability to make decisions in the workplace and society, focusing upon self-interest rather than upon solidarity—these activities produce people on a daily basis; it is the reproduction of the conservatism of everyday life. So we can't ignore the interdependence of socialism as an organic system. Without production for social needs, no real social property; without social property, no worker decision making oriented toward society's needs; without worker decision making, no transformation of people and their needs.

A focus upon a necessary historical sequence (stagism) forgets that the presence of the defects inherited from the old society in any one element poisons the others. And it creates conditions for the restoration of capitalism. *So how is a transition possible when everything depends upon everything else?*

Return to the concept of revolutionary practice—the simultaneous changing of circumstances and human activity or self-change. We have to think not just about changing particular circumstances. To change a structure in which all relations coexist simultaneously and support one another, you have to do more than try to change a few elements in that structure; you must stress at all times the hub of these relations—human beings as subjects and products of their own activity. And how are those people changed? "Only in a revolution," Marx and Engels argued, can the working class "succeed in ridding itself of all the muck of ages and become fitted to found society anew." Revolution is necessary not only to overthrow capital but also to transform human beings "on a mass scale."[3]

But a revolution is not a single act. It is a process—a process of contested reproduction in which the muck of ages itself is constantly being reproduced. The new socialist relation thus advances only by "subordinating all elements of society to itself, or in creating out of it the organs which it still lacks." Precisely because the production of new socialist human beings is an essential aspect of this process, for every concrete measure proposed we must ask two questions: (1) How does this change circumstances?; and (2) How does it help produce revolutionary subjects and increase their capacities?

Here, then, is another common element in all paths to socialism. There is not only the common goal of human development.

There is also the other aspect of the "key link": achieving "our complete development, both individual and collective" is inseparable from practice. Regardless of any differences in paths, *all* paths to socialism necessarily must create the conditions by which people transform themselves through their activity.

A PARTIAL CHARTER
FOR HUMAN DEVELOPMENT

How, then, to begin to talk about making a path to socialism when the paths cannot be identical? We begin by recalling from chapter 2 "the inverse situation" that Marx introduced—the specter of a human society *no longer* subordinated to capital. In short, let us take as our starting point the *inversion* of capitalism, the *negation* of this negation, the inversion of "this inversion, indeed this distortion, which is peculiar to and characteristic of capitalist production."

Capitalism, we know, has its own triangle:

1. Capital owns the means of production, our social heritage, and benefits from this ownership;
2. Under the direction and control of capital, that is, the despotism of the capitalist workplace, workers are exploited, crippled as human beings and alienated from the products of their activity; and
3. Given that the goal that drives production is surplus value, to this end capital destroys human beings and nature, puts workers into competition with each other, and disintegrates families and communities.

Truly a perverse society. Yet, as we have seen, the development of capitalism creates a working class that "by education, tradition and habit" looks upon the requirements of capital as "self-evident natural laws." How is it possible to challenge "this inversion, indeed this distortion" that is contrary to "the worker's own need for development" and to develop an *alternative* common sense?

Insofar as workers do struggle for satisfaction of their needs, that is, are not "apathetic, thoughtless, more or less well-fed instruments of production," they produce themselves as other than simply the products of capital.[4] To go from struggles within the bounds of capitalist relations, though, to those that *break* with the common sense of capitalist relations requires an understanding that capital is inconsistent with the need for full development of our potential.

How can the mass of people move in that direction? One step may be to set out a simple set of propositions, a "Charter for Human Development" that can be recognized as self-evident requirements for human development:

1. Everyone has the right to share in the social heritage of human beings—an equal right to the use and benefits of the products of the social brain and the social hand—in order to be able to develop his or her full potential.
2. Everyone has the right to be able to develop their full potential and capacities through democracy, participation, and protagonism in the workplace and society—a process in which these subjects of activity have the precondition of the health and education that permit them to make full use of this opportunity.
3. Everyone has the right to live in a society in which human beings and nature can be nurtured—a society in which we can develop our full potential in communities based upon cooperation and solidarity.[5]

We are back talking about the "good society"—and the right of everyone to live in such a society. Of course, differing starting points will mean that the concrete measures necessary to achieve such a society will differ in different countries. However, given the universality of the issues posed by such a charter, some of the following measures may be generally applicable.

SUBORDINATING CAPITALIST RELATIONS
OF PRODUCTION

Building a socialist alternative involves subordination of capitalist relations and the creation of new socialist elements. It requires a confrontation not with individual capitals but with the power of capital as a whole. Accordingly, it requires an instrument that can *challenge* the power of capital as a whole, an agency of the working class that can take the power of the state away from capital. With the power of the state, Marx understood, it is possible to convert "*social reason* into *social force*." Indeed, it is the *only* way to build that new society of the associated producers; the change will never occur except through "the transfer of the organised forces of society, viz., the state power, from capitalists and landlords to the producers themselves."[6] Marx understood that you cannot change the world without taking power.

Let us distinguish, then, three hypothetical cases with respect to state power: (1) where the "battle of democracy" has been won (through a revolutionary rupture or a longer process) with the result that state power has been seized from capital and is in the hands of working people; (2) the polar opposite situation where the battle of democracy has hardly been fought and capital rules the existing government; and (3) where the battle of democracy has been fought but not yet won—for example, where a government representing workers has been elected but the balance of forces favors capital.

We begin here with the third case for several reasons. Firstly, this situation was very familiar in the twentieth century and is likely to be characteristic of many countries (especially those of the so-called North) in the twenty-first century. Secondly, the subsequent scenario that unfolded in the twentieth century unfortunately *also* was very familiar—it was the "failure of social democracy" described in *Build It Now* as the process of yielding to and thereby enforcing the logic of capital.[7] Starting from this third case accordingly allows us to stress that there is an *alternative* to the disappointment and betrayal of working people—*a socialist alternative*. Finally, by focusing upon the necessary process of struggle in this third case, it helps to situate the other two scenarios.

We understand the strength of capital. But we also have to grasp its vulnerability—vulnerability because it does not and cannot satisfy the needs of people. Consider, for example, the way capitalism immiserates workers. By alienating workers in the workplace, generating new needs that can fill the vacuum, and keeping wages within the bounds consistent with profitability, "capitalism constantly produces new unsatisfied needs."[8] There is thus a latent antagonism to the corporations whose ownership of the means of production allows them to capture surplus value. With a government oriented toward "the worker's own need for development" that potential hostility can be directed against capital rather than dissipated in wage demands.

CONCRETE MEASURES

Taxing the surplus value that capital secures through its monopoly of the social heritage of human beings is a direct step toward ensuring the right of all to share in the benefits of the products of the social brain and social hand. Furthermore, it allows for the proceeds of these taxes to be used for fighting poverty and developing the education and health opportunities that are a condition for developing the potential of people. Of course, capital has many ways to evade proper taxation. Thus a necessary premise

for achieving this goal is *transparency*—"opening the books" of
the companies to the state in order to permit proper distribution
of the fruits of social production. Ending the secrets of capital is a
definite step toward making social reason into social force. It is
part of the development of a new common sense.

Indeed, "transparency is the rule in the society of associated
producers," and thus its spread is an essential aspect by which the
new world encroaches upon the old.[9] In the workplace, transparency is also required if workers are to develop their capacities
through their protagonism. Opening the books to workers and
giving workers councils the power to act against corruption and
decisions contrary to the needs of workers and society is a key
step.[10] With the power of veto to prevent practices contrary to
health and safety and with a process moving from the right of veto
over supervisors to the right to select their own supervisors,
power in the process of production shifts toward workers.

However, taken only this far, that power remains largely a
defensive power, a right to control the actions of those above, the
right to negate. And, in the absence of the development of the
education and skills of workers to manage production themselves,
the distinction between thinking and doing remains. Therefore
an essential part of creating the conditions for all to develop their
potential and capacities is the *transformation of the workday*.
More than simply a *reduction* of the workday, this is the transformation of the traditional workday to incorporate time for education for worker management.[11] Every workplace, in short, must
become a school of worker management—a place where workers
transform themselves through their practice.

Of course, it is not necessary that the process of worker management be postponed until workers have mastered all the techniques of monitoring financial data and evaluating management
proposals. Generally, workers can already identify the waste
involved in current production processes. Reorganization of production at the base, then, is one of the first areas where workers

can demonstrate the benefits of worker decision making. With their knowledge of existing waste and inefficiency, workers should be able to improve productivity and reduce costs of production. And who benefits from this? By ensuring that the gains from such worker initiatives accrue to enterprise workers and the local community (rather than to enterprises!), a process involving discussions in worker assemblies and community assemblies and forging essential links between workers and community is possible.

How else but through such links between workplaces and communities can consideration of environmental effects and other aspects of communal needs become second nature for workers? Here again transparency and the requirement that local communities have power over local workplaces are an important assault on the power of capital. The development of direct links between workers councils and neighborhood councils, essential organs of cooperation and solidarity for the new society, is a necessary part of the creation of new relations for the collective worker.

SOCIALIST CONDITIONALITY

Extracting surplus value in order to satisfy directly the needs of people, opening the books, introducing worker management—such measures can be shown to flow directly from the above Charter for Human Development. As such, they are conditions that capital should satisfy in order to continue to function at all. But they are not the only examples of socialist conditionality that can be introduced. For example, maintenance of minimum output levels and expanded production of designated necessities (which involves specific investment targets) as well as increased minimum wages (a condition for ensuring the living wages that permit all to share in our common heritage) are further examples of socialist conditionality that can be justified in relation to the need to foster human development.

Of course, none of these measures in themselves change the system. On paper, they look like mere "reforms." Nevertheless, they are *despotic inroads* on the rights of capitalist property. They are part of a process of subordinating capitalism to an alien logic, the logic of human development. Remember the effect of the coexistence of interacting and interpenetrating alien logics. Such measures of "socialist conditionality" are more than reforms precisely because they encroach upon capital and their tendency is to produce crises, system irrationality. *What will happen when capital responds to socialist conditionality by going on strike (refusing to invest, closing down operations, threatening to move)?*

This brings us to what I have called "the sorry history of social democracy, which never ceases to reinforce the capital relation."[12] It is inevitable that capital will respond to despotic inroads on its property rights with capital strikes. Nothing, indeed, is more certain to produce confusion and dismay than *not* anticipating this as capital's reaction. As I argued in *Build It Now*:

> Understanding the responses of capital means that a capital strike can be an opportunity rather than a crisis. If you reject dependence upon capital, the logic of capital can be revealed clearly as contrary to the needs and interests of people. When capital goes on strike, there are two choices, *give* in or *move* in. Unfortunately, social democracy in practice has demonstrated that it is limited by the same things that limit Keynesianism in theory—the givens of the structure and distribution of ownership and the priority of self-interest by the owners. As a result, when capital has gone on strike, the social-democratic response has been to give in.[13]

And, as noted, the effect of the social democratic retreat is to *enforce* the hold of the logic of capital. There is a socialist alternative to a capital strike, however, and that is to *move in*. Its premise is that the workers' government understands capital as the result of exploitation and as the monopolizer of our social heritage and thus is determined to proceed to develop the good society. That is precisely the perspective of the *Communist Manifesto*: "in the beginning," the state introduces measures that "appear economically insufficient and untenable, but which in the course of the movement, outstrip themselves, necessitate further inroads upon the old social order, and are unavoidable as a means of entirely revolutionizing the mode of production."[14] In short, those "despotic inroads" set in motion a process, and the "clear sense is that the process will be self-reinforcing. One measure will always lead on to the next, and 'the proletariat will see itself compelled to go always further.'"[15]

Very simply, as Oscar Lange commented, capitalism requires conditions that "the very existence of a government bent on introducing socialism" will not maintain. "Therefore, the capitalist economy cannot function under a socialist government unless the government is socialist in name only."[16] Thus, in response to the enforcement of socialist conditionality, capital will attempt to remove such a government by all means possible—including subversion, coups, and direct imperialist attack—all as a prelude to the introduction of "grotesquely terroristic laws" for the purpose of restoring the conditions for the reproduction of capitalist relations. The owners of capital thereby demonstrate that they rank the privileges and prerogatives of private ownership higher than ensuring overall human development and reveal to all that there is no alternative for a society based upon the logic of human development than social ownership of the means of production. And so the process in which "the proletariat will see itself compelled to go always further" advances.

THE PLACE OF PRACTICE

The apparent result of this process is that "the proletariat will use its political supremacy to wrest, by degrees, all capital from the bourgeoisie, to centralise all instruments of production in the hands of the State."[17] But where does the element of practice enter into this process? The despotic inroads described above all seem to be initiated and executed by the state. True, the establishment of worker and community assemblies and councils is noted—as is the importance of introducing worker and community decision making. Is this sufficient, though, to produce the new revolutionary subjects, the new socialist human beings capable of going beyond the muck of ages?

If the state and its functionaries are in motion but the people are not, then the effect will be to reproduce the passivity and cynicism characteristic of capitalist society. Rather than the simultaneous changing of circumstances and self-change, what will occur here is similar to that pattern (noted in chapter 2) where "knowledge is a gift bestowed by those who consider themselves knowledgeable upon those whom they consider to know nothing" (Freire). This is the perspective that thinks that it is sufficient to change circumstances in order to change people—which in fact divides society into two parts, one part of which is superior to society (Marx).

A revolutionary state must encourage revolutionary practice. The process outlined above definitely creates the conditions for the mobilization of people against capital. It establishes the basis for national campaigns against capital. However, because the development of self-acting and self-governing movements is an organic process with its own rhythm, the state cannot dictate from above the nature and the pace of the changing of circumstances. Rather, the state must create the enabling framework in which people can transform circumstances and themselves. Decisions on the steps to be taken must therefore flow from meetings and discussions of workers and their communities based upon what they see as their needs. And, since unevenness is inevitable because of differing circumstances and differing histories, uniformity cannot be imposed from above.

Both in their struggle against the continuing resistance of capital and in the creation of the organs of the new society from below, the producers develop their capacities. Accordingly, by creating the legal framework and by supporting unequivocally initiatives from below consistent with that framework (for example, through police and military support for land and workplace occupations and seizures), the state facilitates this process and thereby allows it to advance.[18] It is precisely this interaction between state initiatives and movements from below that nurtures the worker and neighborhood councils that are the basis for a new socialist state—and that advances the development of new socialist men and women.

THE CELLS OF THE NEW

Relatively speaking, it is easy to rupture capitalist property rights and to centralize the means of production in the hands of the state. It is more difficult but *still* relatively easy to create the neighborhood and workers councils that can take increasing control over matters directly affecting them—that is, that can "seize possession of production." *But to what end?* What are the goals of those councils?

Of course, the development of decision making at the level of these new institutions is a process not completed overnight. We understand, though, that this process is essential both for developing the capacities of the producers and also for the emergence of these councils as the elemental cells of the new socialist state, those self-working and self-governing bodies that are no longer subordinate to a state that stands over and above society. Characteristic of these cells is that they foster cooperation and solidarity among their members and, in this respect, point to the characteristics of the new organic system of socialism.

However, they are *only* cells. What connects them? Insofar as these new organs emerge within an old society marked by self-interest and self-orientation, the spontaneous tendency may be to reproduce (as in the case of the nineteenth-century cooperative factories) "all the defects of the existing system." That is, such units may be "mutually indifferent," oriented to group self-interest, and relating to each other on the basis of a *quid pro quo*. In that case, they are not cells of socialism as an organic system "in which all relations coexist simultaneously and support one another." Rather, to the extent that there is "the total isolation of their private interests from one another," they point in the direction of a *different* system, one focused upon group property and exchange relations.

How is it possible to create links between these elemental cells which are based upon the conscious recognition of our interdependence and the right of everyone to the full development of her human potential? As noted in chapter 5, one part of this struggle is the attempt to develop a new common sense, the "new social rationality" based upon the cooperation and solidarity of associated producers. But a "battle of ideas" cannot rest in midair. More is needed than an ideal conception of a socialist alternative; it is also essential to create actual institutions that link those elemental cells on the basis of solidarity and provide a material basis for the new social rationality.

CONNECTING WORKPLACES

Consider, for example, attempting to develop links between *workplaces* (that is, between workers councils). One way in which workplaces may be linked is by connecting suppliers and users in a production chain—a form of vertical integration that can allow rational coordination and planning over a period of time among the participants. Here there is the potential recognition of interdependence and the benefits of cooperation—that is, an extension from what is internal to these units to their combination. *But what would be the basis of this connection between these workplaces?*

If these particular cells are self-oriented and thereby looking to maximize income per member of each individual workforce, planning between these autonomous cells would require extensive discussion and agreement, and that would require an agreement concerning the nature of the *quid pro quo*—that is, the exchange values involved in their transaction. Presumably, these negotiations would be settled where each party to the agreement concluded that it was more beneficial to agree than to abstain. However, it is important to remember that the playing field may not be level. The combination of self-orientation and differential access to particular means of production tells us that this situation is potentially marked by considerable inequality. Here, the more privileged units will have significant advantages in their negotiations with the result that inequality is reinforced.

Such an agreement between self-oriented units would be entirely consistent, too, with intense competition between comparable production chains composed of *other* self-oriented units—and with the attempt to dominate competitors.[19] Further, in the event of any significant change in the economic environment, there would be an incentive for individual units to act in the interests of their own members by defecting from their contractual obligations. And this would always be the bottom line for these cells—the interests of the part rather than the whole. The danger, then, is a reproduction of the Yugoslav experience, because, in itself, a process of planning from below based upon self-oriented producers does not move in the direction of the new social rationality.

In contrast, let us consider an alternative—one that attempts to avoid market relations through the creation of a vertically integrated complex that extends from primary production to the final consumers. An example might be a complex that includes milk production, the processing of milk into milk products and cheese, plastic production for packaging, and a distribution process—with delivery to final consumers in schools and hospitals. As a vertically integrated process, there would be no place for prices in the relationship between steps in this production chain—any more than there is a place for prices for each step of the process of production on a factory production line. Further, individual units within the complex would not have the option of producing and selling to whomever they want. Rather, it is essential that the producers recognize their interdependence and their responsibility to the final consumers.

But how to develop that conscious association of producers? One way would be by recognizing distribution as an essential part of this complex rather than as a specific subdivision of labor. Insofar as distribution of the interim products would be seen as part of the process of production, those engaged in production in any particular stage also would be responsible for bringing their products to subsequent stages—thereby familiarizing themselves with the requirements—quality and the like—and with any waste at these stages.[20] Thus a process of rotation among the producers (so that all are both producers and distributors) would serve to break down the separateness of the various stages in the production chain. Accordingly, a very important part of what is produced in this way is development of knowledge about and a sense of responsibility for the whole. The process, in short, would be one in which every sub-unit is simultaneously a sphere for producing things and also a sphere for developing a sense of unity among the producers.

Yet the real glue that binds this complex together would be responsibility to the final consumer. This is why it is important that the producers have direct contact with those whose needs they are satisfying (in the example above, those in schools and hospitals). Information about the needs of those who depend upon the products is essential in ensuring that adequate production is planned and that the producers understand their responsibility for ensuring that those needs are satisfied. Thus, here again, transparency is essential—transparency about needs and transparency about input requirements. For developing that sense of responsibility, the starting point must be the identification and communication of need rather than the goals of those within the sphere of production. As Mészáros indicated, "The socialist system of incentives is based on the *primacy of needs* over production targets, liberating itself from the tyranny of exchange value."[21]

The needs of society as the starting point are also important when we consider combining units of production horizontally, that is, bringing together the producers in specific localities or sectors. If those cells are focused upon their own self-interest, this will govern any attempt at cooperation among them. Much like cartels or lobby groups, their interests will be served by gaining advantages for their particular combinations, by, for example, restricting competition among themselves in order to raise prices or joining to secure more resources from higher bodies.

Starting from the needs of communities and society, in contrast, guides councils of these productive units to find ways to coordinate their activity, support financially and in kind those communities, and innovate in both products and processes in the interest of serving those needs better. Where the recognized goal is to serve the needs of people, differential access to particular means of production is not a source of inequality. Starting from needs, in short, points to the new organic system of socialism.

CONNECTIONS WITHIN AND BETWEEN COMMUNITIES

Recognition of the primacy of needs points to the importance of creating new organs that express these needs and are a site for the simultaneous changing of circumstances and people—for example, neighborhood councils. Where local associations articulate the needs of their members and develop means for their satisfaction, they produce as a joint product people with altered personalities, people with the capacity to act differently. Combined with a conscious campaign to recognize the right of everyone to the full development of their potential, these new people enter into all their relations as transformed producers.

Thus, like workers councils, neighborhood councils are organs of democracy, participation, and protagonism that transform the actors. Like workers councils, too, their starting point is to organize and work for collective solutions in the interests of their participants. And this is also true when they combine with larger communities to identify and solve problems that go beyond their immediate communities—they are collective efforts dealing with their collective needs.

Certainly these activities build solidarity and community identity while developing our capacities. However, collective *self-interest* remains at the core. And, to the extent that self-interest prevails, the problem of inequality remains. For example, some communities may have benefited particularly from the location of productive, educational, and health facilities dating back to previous periods. How can that inequality be ended so long as particular communities look upon everything they happen to have inherited as their own property? How is such a situation consistent with the above Charter for Human Development, which recognizes the right of everyone to share equally in the use and benefits of our social heritage "in order to be able to develop their full potential"?

Building a solidarian society means going beyond our own particular interests—*or, more accurately, understanding that our particular interest is that we live in a society in which everyone has the right to full human development*. It means that our premise is the concept of a human community. As in the example of the vertically integrated production chain, only when our activity is conscious activity for *others* can we go beyond the infection of self-interest, exchange relations, and inequality.

How, then, to create communities (and a larger community) based upon cooperation and solidarity? Certainly, acts of international solidarity (as in the many exemplary practices of the Cuban Revolution) are important in stressing the needs of others outside one's country, especially since the necessary support is provided without any concept of a quid pro quo. Not only do they change circumstances, but they also are essential for producing people for whom acts of solidarity appear as common sense. Accordingly, they play an important role in the Battle of Ideas.

The essential problem for building the solidarian society, however, is how to incorporate *into communities themselves* the concept of solidarity, so that people produce directly for the needs of others. How, in short, is it possible to make requirements predicated upon the principle of "from each according to his ability, to each according to her need for development" appear to all members of a community as "self-evident natural laws"?

In his *Critique of the Gotha Programme*, Marx was clear that it is the expansion of what a person is entitled to "in his capacity as a member of society" that marks the development of the new society. "*That which is intended for the common satisfaction of needs,*" he pointed out, "such as schools, health services, etc. . . . grows considerably in comparison with present-day society and it grows in proportion as the new society develops." This portion grows once we look upon others as human beings—when we move away from viewing people from "one *definite* side only," where they are "regarded *only as workers* and nothing more is seen in them, everything else being ignored."[22]

To understand what is involved in developing this concept of the entitlement of a person "in his capacity as a member of society," consider the capitalist inversion. The thrust of capital is that we should *pay* for schools (and school supplies), health services (and medical supplies and medicines), and, indeed, everything else that it is possible to commodify. In short, *nothing for people in their capacities as members of society*, everything for them as the owners of money. In contrast, the socialist alternative is to *de*-commodify. *Everything*.

EXPANDING THE COMMONS

As long as we have to *pay* for what we need as individuals, we need money. The question then becomes, how will we obtain that money? If we are not entitled as members of society to obtain what is necessary for the satisfaction of our needs, what gives us entitlement to the money we need? And, if we want more, how do we get more money? It is not a great leap to propose that we should get money in accordance with our efforts, our contribution, the contribution of our present *and* past labor—all concepts based upon labor power, the personal condition of production, as our property. This is how the old society is reproduced.

Obviously, as Marx understood, we enter the new society "economically, morally and intellectually, still stamped with the birthmarks of the old society." Those institutions and conceptions cannot be banished overnight. Thus the question is how to make "despotic inroads" on these rights of property. Is there any way other than by separating use-values from exchange values, that is, by expanding the commons? Any way other than by expanding systematically that which we are entitled to as human beings, in our capacity as members of society?

Besides adequate schools and health services, there are many other premises for the development of people that can be made available to them as members of communities. Transit, food, shelter—all are requirements of people that could be the common property of the community. These can be introduced on a step-by-step basis in communities, and each step can strengthen both the communal institutions and the sense of solidarity within those communities. All this is part of a process of creating a new common sense, one in which expansion of the commons to provide more of people's needs in a non-commodity form as well as the taxation of capital to support the new distribution relations are increasingly seen as self-evident natural laws.

Won't the expansion of common property, however, generate the theoretical result stressed by conservative ideologists that rational (that is, self-oriented) individuals will produce collective irrationality (such as exhaustion of scarce resources) where common property rights exist? Is a "tragedy of the commons" inevitable? In fact, there is considerable evidence that common property in practice has been successfully managed (in terms of efficiency and equity) by communities. Focusing in particular on the experience with natural resources to which all members of a community have access (fisheries, irrigation systems, forests, and the like), many studies have stressed the norms, conventions, and working rules by which such communities (for example, indigenous communities) have successfully managed the commons.[23]

The key is the existence of communal institutions—formal or informal arrangements by which common property is monitored and which provide sanctions for the abuse of the common interest by individuals. Those communal institutions can be effective because (in contrast to the premise of neoclassical economics that the unit of analysis is the atomistic individual with neither past nor future), the individuals in these communities "have shared a past and expect to share a future. It is important," Elinor Ostrom notes, "for individuals to maintain their reputations as reliable members of the community."[24] Insofar as the community (which is small enough to allow easy monitoring and sanctioning) is able to administer the commons, its institutions (such as neighborhood councils) are strengthened through this process.

Expanding the commons acknowledges everyone's right to human development, and it thus produces social individuals who recognize their interdependence. But where will the resources that constitute the commons in each community come from? In part, they will come from local workplaces as contributions to the community and from the collective work within the community itself. And, depending upon the particular communities, they may be made available from elsewhere (other communities) and from the existing state. The solidarian society develops organically by beginning at the neighborhood and community level, but it continues only by building solidarity directly between rich and poor communities—both within and between individual nations. And that, too, is an important part of the process of building rich human beings.

The process of building a path to socialism involves the development and deepening of a new social relation—that of associated producers who relate to each other on the basis of communality. In this process, the producers (a) rupture capitalist property rights and establish social ownership of the means of production, (b) "seize possession" of production and transform it into a protagonistic process in which their capacities expand, and (c) produce use-values in accordance with the need of everyone for the opportunity to develop her full potential. Every step of this process is a process of struggle.

7. Developing a Socialist Mode of Regulation

Each aspect of the process of "becoming" of socialism involves an encroachment upon capital. Yet, as noted in chapter 5, until such time as the associated producers develop a specifically socialist mode of production, all the inroads made by the invading socialist society remain contingent. Indeed, only struggle will ensure that the continued existence of elements inherited from capitalism does not lead to reversal of those inroads.

Given the tendency for systemic incoherence and crises inherent in the combination of alien elements characteristic of the becoming of socialism, the threat to the new socialist society is always present. Not only the counter-revolution implicit in the remaining outposts of capitalist ownership of the means of production. And not only the tendency of bureaucrats and managers to usurp the protagonistic democracy of the producers in workplaces and communities and thereby to "seize possession of production" for themselves. But also the tendency to resolve problems and inefficiencies by turning to the logic of the market.

Precisely because of the need to struggle to ensure that the invading socialist society continues to advance, we have insisted that the development of a "socialist mode of regulation" is essential. That mode of regulation must achieve consciously what a specifically socialist mode of production will tend to do spontaneously—ensure the reproduction of socialist relations of production (as represented by the socialist triangle). In short, the socialist mode of regulation supports the inroads of the new socialist society during the period in which the associated producers begin to alter the mode of production into one that serves their needs.

The socialist mode of regulation encompasses, firstly, the Battle of Ideas—the ideological struggle oriented toward human development. It thus stresses the perversion of capitalism, the importance of democratic, participatory, and protagonistic practice in workplaces and communities, and the emphasis upon a new social rationality based upon cooperation and solidarity. Secondly, it involves the creation of institutions like workers councils and neighborhood councils, which are essential instruments for developing new socialist subjects through their practice. Finally, this mode of regulation requires a state that supports this struggle ideologically, economically, and militarily and thus serves as the midwife for the birth of the new society.

But what do we mean by the state? We have talked about *two* states here—one, the state that workers captured at the outset and that initiates despotic inroads upon capital, that is, the *old* state; and, second, the emerging new state based upon workers councils and neighborhood councils as its cells. The starting point, of course, is with the old state, and the becoming of socialism as an organic system is a process of transition from the old state to the new. But this means that the two must coexist and interact throughout this process of becoming.

Both that "engine of despotism," with that "ready-made state machinery" characterized by a "systematic and hierarchic division of labour," and the participatory and protagonistic state from below, accordingly form part of that socialist mode of regulation that must support the new relations based upon the associated producers. The inherent tension between these two states—between the top-down orientation from within the old state and the bottom-up emphasis of the workers and community councils—is obvious. Yet that tension is not the principal contradiction.

Given the significant presence within the old state of revolutionary actors who are committed to building the new society, it would be an error to treat the old state as if it were no different from the capitalist state. Similarly, given the effects of the "education, tradition and habit" of those formed within the old society, we should not be surprised at the power of the old ideas to undermine efforts to build the new state from below. Thus, both within the cells of the new state and within the structures of the old state, there is an inevitable struggle between those who are working to build the new society and those who are content with the old (either because of inertia or because of existing privileges).

So it would appear that there is a clear basis for connecting revolutionaries at both levels, in both states. However, wouldn't such a link be incoherent and unstable—given the profound difference in the two states? In fact, the interaction between the two states is essential. Each has a necessary part in a socialist mode of regulation. The old state can see the picture as a whole at the outset; thus it is well situated to identify critical bottlenecks and places for initiatives that require a concentration of forces (including actions to defend the process militarily against internal and external enemies determined to reverse every inroad). However, as might be expected from its heritage, this state has the tendency to act from above, to choose expedience over the process of revolutionary practice—that is, to divide society into two parts, one part of which is superior to society.[1]

In contrast, the cells of the new state, which are the space for human development through practice, can identify the needs and capacities of people and can mobilize people to link those needs and capacities directly. Further, precisely because this is where transparency is most effective, the councils in workplaces and communities can police waste, sabotage, and other attempts to reverse the process. However, the initial focus of these cells inevitably will be one of localism. And, since the links to other communities and workplaces only develop through practice, it takes time before the concept of the whole develops organically in these units. In short, although the course of development of socialism as an organic system requires the creation of those links between cells, that process cannot be instantaneous; accordingly, the new state is not capable at the outset of making essential decisions that require concentration and coordination of forces.

Thus, though the process of development is one in which the old state yields to the new, the two contradictory states (by origin and orientation) complement each other in building socialism. Isolated, these two states inherently lead to deformations, but the process advances through the combination of the revolutionary elements within each—in short, by walking on two legs.

But how can the old state foster the development of the new—rather than cause it to be stillborn?

THE IMPORTANCE OF "SOCIALIST ACCOUNTANCY"

To build the new socialist society, it is necessary to develop new, socialist concepts. We cannot proceed as if the categories and concepts of capitalism are applicable to the relations of associated producers (any more than the specifically capitalist mode of production or the capitalist state). Indeed, the Battle of Ideas requires the development of concepts that support social rationality over the rationality of the logic of capital.

As an alternative to the particular rationality embodied in the accounting and administration characteristic of the logic of capital, Istvan Mészáros introduced the term "socialist accountancy" in his *Beyond Capital*.[2] Socialist accountancy, he proposed, has as its "fundamental principle," *quality* (as opposed to capital's focus upon quantity) and has a direct relation to needs. Thus the shift to "the *qualitative* determinations of social accountancy" involves the "radical reorientation of production towards use-value"—use-values not in the abstract but for the social individuals produced within the new community.[3]

In his subsequent work, *The Challenge and Burden of Historical Time*, Mészáros returned to the concept of socialist accountancy and stressed another side—the importance of "free time," "disposable time," time that can be put to creative use by "self-realizing individuals."[4] Ending "the tyranny of *necessary labor-time*," he proposed, is the condition for "the conscious adoption and creative use of *disposable* time as the orienting principle of societal reproduction."[5] Thus production for needs, that alternative rationality of socialist accountancy, has as its premise the negation of necessary labor time: "The production of free time in the course of history," Mészáros notes, is "the necessary condition of emancipation." We need, in short, to end the situation characteristic of capitalism in which "*time is everything, man is nothing; he is at most time's carcase.*"[6]

A concept of socialist accountancy is certainly essential to break with capitalist accountancy and capital's concept of efficiency. In contrast to Mészáros's focus upon needs, disposable labor and free time, however, the starting point in this book has been the "key link" of human development and practice; as a result, the concept of socialist accountancy offered here differs. With the focus upon revolutionary practice, that simultaneous changing of circumstance and self-change, we can never forget that all human activity generates joint products. The focus upon socialist accountancy here stresses the change in *both* products— the change in circumstances and the change in human capacities.

In short, rather than capitalist accountancy, which focuses upon the time of production and a concept of efficiency that looks at output per unit of labor in the production of *things*, a socialist alternative recognizes that the development of the capacities of workers is an essential *investment in human beings*. A concept of "socialist efficiency" must incorporate explicitly the effects upon human capacities of all activities.

Take, for example, the obvious example of the transformation of the traditional workday to include several hours a day of instruction in worker management. We have seen that this change in the concept of work is critical for the development of the capacities of the producers. If the effect of this change upon workers is not considered explicitly, however, this shift necessarily appears as inefficient compared to the output previously produced during the traditional workday. However, this change is clearly an investment for the future—an investment in human capacities. Indeed, *every* new process of participation and protagonism is a process of learning and thus investment; the joint product created is new subjects with new capacities who enter into all their relations as these new subjects.

Compare that to the result of capitalist relations of production. As discussed in chapter 2, "The joint product of capitalist production that Marx identified in *Capital* is the fragmented, crippled human being whose enjoyment consists in possessing and consuming things." With socialist accountancy, we understand that such a result must be entered as *negative* in the account books and in our calculations of efficiency. The same must be said of the effect upon human capacities of *any* hierarchical forms that preserve an "alienated command structure" that prevents the "full development of the creative potentialities of the social individuals."[7]

It is easy to remain a prisoner of conceptions appropriate to capitalist relations. This is true with respect to the concept of the workday, the concept of production (as noted in chapter 2), the concepts of wealth (chapter 1), and of productive and unproductive labor.[8] By taking seriously the development of concepts appropriate not to capitalism but to socialism, though, we arm

ourselves in the struggle to build new socialist relations. The concept of socialist accountancy directs us to stress the development
of institutions through which people can develop their capacities
through their practice. It is in this respect essential for freeing us
from the apparent rationality of capitalist concepts, thereby helping to foster the new organs of revolutionary practice that the
socialist society requires.

Capitalist accounting, though, points in the opposite direction. It neither measures the investments in human capacities that
are the result of people working together and learning how to take
collective control of their affairs (because these are essentially
non-monetary), nor does it consider the costs of bypassing the
organic development of such institutions. Precisely because capitalist accountancy doesn't think about the simultaneous changing
of circumstance and self-change and about the joint products of
activity, it is biased toward commandist expediency, such as top-
down state decisions and managerial authority in the workplace.
The effects upon the development of the capacities of people in
such cases are predictable.[9]

However, when the elements of the new state have not been
developed, the tendency inherent in the old state will be to solve
problems from above. That is precisely why a clear conception of
the importance of socialist accountancy and rationality is necessary in shaping all policy decisions. The Battle of Ideas, the
emerging cells of the new socialist state, and an old state that aids
in its own demise by embracing policies oriented specifically to
the development of the capacities of socialist human beings—all
of these are the components of a socialist mode of regulation
which can succeed in the struggle of contested reproduction.

Take, for example, the disease of consumerism we inherit
from capitalism. How else but through the Battle of Ideas can we
ideologically challenge this pattern? How else but by insisting
upon a concept of human development that is not the accumulation of things but the development of rich human beings? How

else but by struggling to make the right of everyone to develop their full potential common sense? But can this be done without the worker management and community decision making that end the alienating and emptying process of production character-istic of capitalism, thereby undermining the material basis of con-sumerism? Also, can this pattern be challenged without the emerging institutions of the new state that can foster and monitor the alternative basis of distribution, the expansion of the com-mons? And can those new relations of distribution be preserved without the protection and support of the old state?

This is a struggle of contested reproduction. In this period before socialism has developed upon its own foundations, a socialist mode of regulation is essential to prevent the restoration of capitalism (or the emergence of productive relations where the associated producers do not possess production themselves). Precisely because elements of differing organic systems coexist and interact, systemic incoherence will generate problem after problem—crises but also opportunities. The central point is not that the problems are present but rather how much depends upon the nature of the response to them.

How, for example, can a society attempting to build socialism deal with the problem of shortages (the result of either rising demand or lagging supply)? There is a critical difference between the social rationality of socialism and the atomistic individual rationality of capitalism (one that reflects the gap between social-ist accountancy and capitalist accountancy).[10] Social rationality calls for discussions within communities and workplaces in order to explore how to economize on the use of the product in short supply and also how to expand its output and availability. Social rationality thus makes the collective worker a subject in the pro-cess of thinking and doing in the search for solutions.

In contrast, focus upon individual rationality resolves the pro-blem of shortage in two ways. On the one hand, by increasing the price of the product in question and forcing every person to make an individually rational decision—for example, to reduce its use, to substitute another product in its place, or to find a way to secure additional income in order to maintain or increase current consumption levels. On the other hand, this market rationality stresses the use of increasing monetary incentives to encourage greater efficiency and production on the part of workers. In general, in this conception of rationality, atomistic individuals respond to price signals that stand outside them; communal needs and communal purposes are the least of their concerns. This individual rationality is *social irrationality*.

Each of these two approaches, of course, produces more than a solution to a problem of shortage. Recall the process of revolutionary practice—every activity changes not only circumstances but also the actors. In short, we always have to ask what the joint product is. What kind of people are produced? In this case, the answer is quite clear. In contrast to the way social rationality reinforces the idea that the necessary solutions are communal in nature, individual rationality reinforces the idea of the old society— that solutions are individual and that the real way to resolve problems is to obtain more money on an individual basis.

Without a concept that transcends capital, the responses to the inevitable problems that emerge in this period of contested reproduction will reproduce capitalist rationality. By the calculus of socialist accounting, social rationality produces the people who are fit to build the new society—clearly a positive effect not captured by capitalist accounting. In contrast, individual rationality may generate efficient solutions from the perspective of capitalist accounting; however, through the lens of socialist accounting, the measurement is negative. Solutions relying upon individual rationality produce people who are fit to produce a society that is not socialist—and this is what a socialist mode of regulation must prevent.

FINALLY, THE PARTY

A socialist mode of regulation doesn't of course drop from the sky. The Battle of Ideas, the emergence of the new state and the direction of the old state, are not the product of spontaneity. Precisely because the new society is economically, morally, and intellectually marked by what has been inherited from the old society, there will never be a spontaneous process whereby all the producers simultaneously grasp the need for socialism.

Very simply, there is a need for leadership in the struggle for socialism. But what kind of leadership is needed to build a process based upon the key link of human development and practice? What kind of leadership is essential to build socialism for the twenty-first century?[11] Obviously, it must be a leadership that creates the conditions whereby people can develop their capacities, the conditions of participation and protagonism necessary to "ensure their complete development, both individual and collective."

Obviously, this cannot be the work of an individual leader. Collective leaders, active throughout the society, are necessary to unite the collective worker. As I argued several years ago in relation to the political implications of my *Beyond CAPITAL*, given the heterogeneity of the collective worker (and its various forms of immiseration) and capital's use of differences to divide the working class in order to defeat it, a political instrument is needed to mediate among the parts of the collective worker, provide the welcoming space where popular movements can learn from each other and develop the unity necessary to defeat capital.[12] Illustrating this point concretely, *Build It Now* made the following argument in relation to current developments in Venezuela:

Given the enemies of the Bolivarian Revolution (both those outside and inside it), a political instrument which can bring together those fighting for protagonistic democracy in the workplace and in the community is needed. One which can develop and articulate common demands like that of transparency (a necessary condition both for real democracy and for fighting corruption). One based not upon narrow groupings but upon all the popular organizations and representing the interests of the working class as a whole.

How else can the inherent contradictions among those who want the revolution to continue—e.g., contradictions between the informal sector and the formal sector, between the exploited and the excluded, between workers and peasants, between cooperatives and state sectors—be resolved except through democratic discussion, persuasion, and education that begins from the desire for unity in struggle? How else can you prevent contradictions among the people from becoming contradictions between the people and the enemy—except by the creation of a party for the future of the Revolution (rather than its past)? A party from below which can continue the process of revolutionary democracy that is needed to build this new type of socialism.[13]

But what kind of political instrument can build such a process? Only a party of a different type. Nothing could be more contrary to a theory that stresses the self-development of the working class through revolutionary practice than a party that sees itself as superior to social movements and as the place where the masses of members are meant to learn the merits of discipline in following the decisions made by infallible central committees.[14]

On the contrary, once we focus upon the transformative effect of popular struggles, we understand that, rather than coming to grassroots movements with preconceived plans, the point is to learn from them and to spread that understanding. "The political instrument's role," Marta Harnecker has stressed, "is to facilitate, not to supersede. We have to fight to eliminate any sign of verticalism which cancels out people's initiative because popular participation is not something that can be decreed from above."[15]

Further, understanding the way in which hierarchical structures can sap the creative energy and enthusiasm of those committed to the struggle to put an end to capital points to the need to make the base of any party structure the space for initiatives. Rather than the insistence upon uniform forms of participation (in the workplace or community), the possibility of autonomous collectives and affinity groups organized according to their interests. Rather than information and instructions passing vertically, the sharing and emulation of ideas and experiences horizontally. Rather than a single line of march in this asymmetrical warfare against capital, guerrilla units functioning under a general line and understanding the need for unity in struggle for major battles—how else to unleash creative energy and foster the revolutionary practice that can produce the people who can defeat capital?

But think about this relationship between a political instrument and the movements from below. It is clearly not a hierarchical, verticalist relationship. The leadership that a political instrument can provide fosters revolutionary practice only by continuously learning from below. There is, in short, a process of interaction, a dialectic between the political instrument and popular movements. By itself, the former becomes a process of command from above; by itself, the latter cannot develop a concept of the whole—that is, it cannot transcend localism. In short, articulation of the two is essential—another case of the necessity to walk on two legs.

We need to learn from experience. The effect of hierarchy and transmission belts in deforming the socialist experiments of the twentieth century should be clear to all. That is not an experience to repeat in the twenty-first century. As I argued in *Build It Now*, in the same way that Marx was prepared to change his own views in the light of the Paris Commune, we have to think about socialism now in the light of the experiences of the twentieth century:

We need to understand that socialism of the twentieth century cannot be a statist society where decisions are top-down and where all initiative is the property of state office-holders or cadres of self-reproducing vanguards. Precisely because socialism focuses upon human development, it stresses the need for a society that is democratic, participatory, and protagonistic. A society dominated by an all-powerful state does not produce the human beings who can create socialism.[16]

THE OTHER TWO SCENARIOS

The need for a political instrument that facilitates the process whereby people can transform both society and themselves is not limited to the situation "where the battle of democracy has been fought but not yet won—for example, where a government representing workers has been elected but the balance of forces favors capital." We have considered some characteristics of that scenario, the third case introduced in the last chapter. But what about the other cases that we posed?

Consider the first case, "where the 'battle of democracy' has been won (through a revolutionary rupture or a longer process) with the result that state power has been seized from capital and is in the hands of working people." How would the process of building socialism differ from the case we have explored? In fact, almost everything already posed must be reproduced in this case. Why? Simply because *a revolutionary rupture in itself is not at all the same as creating a state that is in the hands of working people.*

The state may no longer be in the hands of capital, but that doesn't mean it is in the hands of the associated producers. The same is true of the means of production. Indeed, in the absence of the development of the workers and community councils that are cells of the new society of the associated producers, a *different* social relation possesses both the state and the means of production.[17] Clearly, focus upon elements such as that key link of human development and practice and on the struggle for a specifically socialist mode of regulation is essential in this case as well.

What about the second case, the "situation where the battle of democracy has hardly been fought and capital rules the existing government"? Obviously, the struggle for human development cannot wait until an election has been won. On the contrary, that struggle is essential for changing the balance of forces. As Marx stressed, it is only through their struggles that workers produce themselves as other than "apathetic, thoughtless, more or less well-fed instruments of production." Workers who renounce wage struggles, for example, "disqualify themselves for the initiating of any larger movement."[18]

Once again, we can return to the elements of the invading socialist society discussed earlier. Demands around which to organize for human development while capital controls the existing government may include (in no special order):

1. Increasing taxes upon capital for the purpose of expanding production of the goods and services essential for human development;

2. Increasing minimum wages to ensure that everyone can meet minimum conditions for sharing in civilization;

3. Opening the books of corporations to government and workers;

4. Introducing health and safety regulations that ensure that workers can veto any practices harmful to health;

5. Shortening the workday to provide workers with the time to develop their potential through education and to participate in local community work;

6. Ensuring community control over productive practices of workplaces in their localities in order to prevent environmental destruction and conditions harmful to health;

7. Creation of democratic, participatory, and protagonistic

institutions in workplaces and communities that ensure the "complete development, individual and collective," of all members of society;

8. Expansion of the commons—decommodify so that all that is necessary for human development is available for everyone in their capacity as members of society;

9. Determination of "socialist conditionality," the minimum conditions that capital must meet at a given time in order to continue to exist.

All of these can be part of campaigns that can change both circumstances and the actors, thereby helping to build a force that can struggle to build a socialist society. Yet it is essential that these not be seen as separate and distinct demands—because then they become simply partial reforms. Rather, it is necessary to understand the connections between these questions—how they are all aspects of a socialist society, all different sides of the struggle for "the worker's own need for development."

This is where the concept of a Charter for Human Development (introduced in the preceding chapter) can be especially useful; it shows the unity of these separate demands:

1. Everyone has the right to share in the social heritage of human beings, has an equal right to the use and benefits of the products of the social brain and the social hand, in order to be able to develop his or her full potential.

2. Everyone has the right to be able to develop their full potential and capacities through democracy, participation and protagonism in the workplace and society—a process in which these subjects of activity have the precondition of the health and education which permits them to make full use of this opportunity.

3. Everyone has the right to live in a society in which human beings and nature can be nurtured—a society in which we

can develop our full potential in communities based upon cooperation and solidarity.

In the struggle against capitalism, a system that destroys human beings and nature, we need a vision of an alternative. And we need to understand the only way that that vision can be made real. The focus upon human development and practice, the key link, offers a vision of a good society oriented toward the development of rich human beings. And that, after all, is the socialist alternative—real human development.

Bibliography

Bettelheim, Charles. *Economic Calculation and Forms of Property: An Essay on the Transition between Capitalism and Socialism.* New York: Monthly Review Press, 1975.

Bromley, Daniel W., ed. *Making the Commons Work: Theory, Practice, Policy.* San Francisco: ICS Press, 1992.

Bruce, Iain. *The Real Venezuela: Making Socialism in the 21st Century.* London: Pluto Press, 2008.

Devine, Pat. *Democracy and Economic Planning: The Political Economy of a Self-Governing Society.* Boulder: Westview Press, 1988.

Freire, Paolo. *Pedagogy of the Oppressed.* New York: Continuum, 2006.

Harnecker, Marta. *Rebuilding the Left.* London: Zed Books, 2007.

Hegel, G.W.F. *The Phenomenology of Mind.* New York: Harper Torchbooks, 1967.

Horvat, Branko. *The Political Economy of Socialism.* Armonk, N.Y.: M. E. Sharpe, 1982.

Horvat, Branko. *Towards a Theory of Planned Economy.* Beograd: Yugoslav Institute of Economic Research, 1964.

Lange, Oscar. *On the Economic Theory of Socialism,* edited by Benjamin Lippincott. New York: McGraw Hill, 1964.

Lebowitz, Michael A. "Building on Defects: Theses on the Misinterpretation of Marx's Gotha Critique." *Science and Society* (October 2007).

_____. "Contradictions in the 'Lower Phase' of Communist Society." *Socialism in the World* 59 (Belgrade, 1987).

_____. "El pueblo y la propriedad en la construccion del comunismo." *Marx Ahora: Revista Internacional* 16 (Havana, 2003).

_____. "Kornai and the Vanguard Mode of Production." *Cambridge Journal of Economics* 24/3 (May 2000).

_____. "La acumulacion originaria de relaciones comunistas." *Marx Ahora: Revista Internacional* 11 (Havana, 2001).

_____. "New Wings for Socialism." *Monthly Review* (April 2007).

_____. "The Capitalist Workday, the Socialist Workday." *MRZine* (April 2008).

_____. "The Politics of Assumption, the Assumption of Politics." *Historical Materialism* 14/2 (June 2006).

_____. "The Politics of *Beyond CAPITAL.*" *Historical Materialism* 14/4 (2006).

_____. "The Socialist Fetter Considered." Paper presented to the Union of Radical Political Economists at ASSA in New Orleans, January 1992.

_____. "The Socialist Fetter: A Cautionary Tale." In *The Socialist Register 1991,* edited by Ralph Miliband and Leo Panitch. London: Merlin, 1991.

_____. "Trapped Inside a Box? Five Questions for Ben Fine." *Historical Materialism* 18/1 (2010).

_____. *Beyond CAPITAL: Marx's Political Economy of the Working Class.* 2nd ed. New York: Palgrave Macmillan, 2003.

_____. *Build It Now: Socialism for the Twenty-first Century.* New York: Monthly Review Press, 2006.

_____. *Following Marx: Method, Critique and Crisis.* Leiden: Brill, 2009.

Lenin, V. I. *The Right of Nations to Self-Determination, Lenin: Selected Works.* Vol. 1. Moscow: Progress Publishers, 1967.

_____. *The State and Revolution.* Peking: Foreign Languages Press, 1965.

Lipietz, Alain. "Reflections on a Tale: The Marxist Foundations of the Concepts of Regulation and Accumulation" *Studies in Political Economy* 26 (Summer 1988).

_____. *Mirages and Miracles: The Crises of Global Fordism.* London: Verso, 1987.

Marx, Karl, and Frederick Engels. *Collected Works.* Vol. 30. New York:

International Publishers.

_____. *The Communist Manifesto.* In Marx and Engels, *Collected Works.* Vol. 6. New York: International Publishers, 1976.

_____. *The German Ideology.* In Marx and Engels, *Collected Works.* Vol. 5. New York: International Publishers, 1976.

Marx, Karl. "Comments on James Mill." In Marx and Engels, *Collected Works.* Vol. 3. New York: International Publishers, 1975.

_____. "First Outline of *The Civil War in France.*" In Marx and Engels, *On the Paris Commune.* Moscow: Progress Publishers, 1971.

_____. "Inaugural Address of the Working Men's International Association." In Marx and Engels, *Collected Works.* Vol. 20. New York: International Publishers, 1985.

_____. "Instructions to the Delegates of the Provisional General Council. The Different Questions." In *Minutes of the General Council of the First International, 1864–66.* Moscow: Foreign Languages Publishing House, n.d.

_____. "On the Jewish Question." In Marx and Engels, *Collected Works.* Vol. 3. New York: International Publishers, 1975.

_____. "Theses on Feuerbach." In Marx and Engels, *Collected Works.* Vol. 6. New York: International Publishers, 1976.

_____. *Capital.* Vol. 1. New York: Vintage Books, 1977.

_____. *Capital.* Vol. 3. New York: Vintage Books, 1981.

_____. *Critique of the Gotha Programme.* In Marx and Engels, *Selected Works.* Vol. 2. Moscow: Foreign Languages Publishing House, 1962.

_____. *Economic and Philosophical Manuscripts of 1844.* In Marx and Engels, *Collected Works.* Vol. 3. New York: International Publishers, 1975.

_____. *Economic Manuscript of 1861–63 Conclusion.* In Marx and Engels, *Collected Works.* Vol. 34. New York: International Publishers, 1994.

_____. *Economic Manuscript of 1861–63.* In Marx and Engels, *Collected Works.* Vol. 30. New York: International Publishers, 1988.

_____. *Grundrisse.* New York: Vintage Books, 1973.

_____. *The Civil War in France.* In Marx and Engels, *On the Paris Commune.* Moscow: Progress Publishers, 1971.

_____. *The Poverty of Philosophy.* In Marx and Engels, *Collected Works.* Vol. 6. New York: International Publishers, 1976.

_____. *Theories of Surplus Value.* Vol. 3. Moscow: Progress
     Publishers, 1971.

Mészáros, István. *Beyond Capital: Toward a Theory of Transition.* New
     York: Monthly Review Press, 1994.

_____. *The Challenge and Burden of Historical Time: Socialism in the
     Twenty-first Century.* New York: Monthly Review Press,
     2008.

Ostrom, Elinor. *Governing the Commons: The Evolution of Institutions
     for Collective Action.* Cambridge: Cambridge University Press,
     1990.

Preobrazhensky, Evgeny. *The New Economics.* Oxford: Clarendon
     Press, 1965.

Sen, Amartya. *Inequality Reexamined.* Cambridge: Harvard University
     Press, 1992.

Sève, Lucien. *Man in Marxist Theory and the Psychology of
     Personality.* Sussex: Harvester Press, 1978.

Shanin, Teodor. *Late Marx and the Russian Road: Marx and "The
     Peripheries of Capitalism."* New York: Monthly Review Press,
     1983.

Smith, Adam. *The Wealth of Nations.* New York: Modern Library,
     1937.

Soviet Constitution of 1936. Available at
     http://www.departments.bucknell.edu/russian/const/36cons0
     1.html.

Tablada, Carlos. *Che Guevara: Economics and Politics in the
     Transition to Socialism.* Sydney: Pathfinder, 1989.

Tito, Jose. Broz. "Factories to the Workers." *Socialist Thought and
     Practice* 15/6 (Belgrade, June 1975).

Notes

INTRODUCTION

1. Michael A. Lebowitz, *Build It Now: Socialism for the Twenty-First Century* (New York: Monthly Review Press, 2006), 53–60.
2. Karl Marx, *Grundrisse* (New York: Vintage Books, 1973), 488, 541, 708.
3. For references to the Bolivarian Constitution, see Lebowitz, *Build It Now*, 72, 89–90.
4. Karl Marx and Frederick Engels, *Collected Works*, vol. 30 (New York: International Publishers), 190–92.
5. Karl Marx, *Capital*, vol. 3 (New York: Vintage Books, 1981), 367.
6. Karl Marx, *The Poverty of Philosophy,* in Marx and Engels, *Collected Works*, vol. 6 (New York: International Publishers, 1976), 167; Marx, *Grundrisse*, 278.
7. Karl Marx, *Capital*, vol. 1 (New York: Vintage Books, 1977), 718, 716.
8. Ibid., 724.
9. Ibid., 935.
10. See chapter 2 for a discussion of alienating production under capitalism.
11. Marx, *Capital*, vol. I, 899.
12. Michael A. Lebowitz, *Beyond CAPITAL: Marx's Political Economy of the Working Class,* 2nd ed. (New York: Palgrave Macmillan, 2003), 177.
13. Marx, *Grundrisse*, 158.
14. Lebowitz, *Beyond CAPITAL*, 203, 209.

15. Karl Marx, *"First Outline of the Civil War in France,"* in Karl Marx
     and Frederick Engels, *On the Paris Commune* (Moscow: Progress
     Publishers, 1971), 149-50, 154; Lebowitz, *Beyond CAPITAL,*
     193-95.

16. Lebowitz, *Build It Now,* 109.

17. Ibid., 90-92.

18. Ibid., 100. *Alo Presidente* transcripts are available online.

19. István Mészáros, *Beyond Capital: Toward a Theory of Transition*
     (New York: Monthly Review Press, 1994), 750-51, 757-60.

20. Lebowitz, *Build It Now,* 108-9.

21. Michael A. Lebowitz, "New Wings for Socialism," *Monthly Review,*
     April 2007.

22. Mészáros, *Beyond Capital,* 823.

23. Ibid., 833-84, 845.

24. Lebowitz, *Build It Now,* 67, 68.

CHAPTER 1. THE WEALTH OF PEOPLE

1.   Marx, *Capital,* vol. 1, 753, 756-77.

2.   Ibid., vol. 1, 443.

3.   Marx, *Grundrisse,* 528.

4.   Ibid., 528.

5.   Adam Smith, *Wealth of Nations* (New York: Modern Library, 1937),
     13; Marx, *Economic Manuscript of 1861-63* in Karl Marx and
     Frederick Engels, *Collected Works,* vol. 30 (New York: International
     Publishers, 1988), 255, 277.

6.   Marx, *Grundrisse,* 585; Karl Marx and Frederick Engels, *The
     German Ideology,* in Marx and Engels, *Collected Works,* vol. 5 (New
     York: International Publishers, 1976), 48.

7.   Lebowitz, *Beyond CAPITAL,* 85.

8.   Marx, *Economic Manuscript of 1861-63,* vol. 30, 260.

9.   Marx, *Grundrisse,* 694, 704-6; Marx, *Capital,* vol. 3, 175.

10. Marx, *Grundrisse,* 700, 704, 706.

11. Marx and Engels, *The German Ideology,* 47-48.

12. Marx, *Grundrisse,* 585.

13. Marx, *Capital,* vol. 1, 757.

14. Marx, *Grundrisse,* 694; Lebowitz, *Beyond CAPITAL,* 156-57.

15. Lebowitz, *Beyond CAPITAL,* 45.

16. See the discussion of the perspective of individual capitalists in con-
     trast to the necessary conditions for reproduction of capital as a whole
     in "The Fallacy of Everyday Notions," in Michael A. Lebowitz,
     Following Marx: Method, Critique and Crisis (Leiden: Brill, 2009),
     chap. 1.

17. Marx, *Capital*, vol. 1, 680; Lebowitz, *Beyond CAPITAL*, 172–75.

18. For a discussion of the inherent tendency of capital to increase the degree of separation among workers, see Lebowitz, *Beyond CAPITAL*, 101–19, 216; and Michael A. Lebowitz, "The Politics of Assumption, the Assumption of Politics," *Historical Materialism*, 14/2 (June 2006), revised in Lebowitz, *Following Marx*, chap. 19.

19. Karl Marx, *Economic Manuscript of 1861–63 (Conclusion),* in Marx and Engels, *Collected Works*, vol. 34 (New York: International Publishers, 1994), 32–33.

20. Marx, *Capital*, vol. 1, 899.

21. Lebowitz, *Beyond CAPITAL,* especially chaps 5, 7 and 8.

22. Pat Devine, *Democracy and Economic Planning: The Political Economy of a Self-Governing Society* (Boulder: Westview Press, 1988).

23. Charles Bettelheim, *Economic Calculation and Forms of Property: An Essay on the Transition between Capitalism and Socialism* (New York: Monthly Review Press, 1975), 111.

24. This question is explored in Michael A. Lebowitz, "People and Property in the Building of Communism," presented to the conference, "The Work of Karl Marx and the Challenges of the 21st Century," in Havana, 5–8 May 2003 and published as "El pueblo y la propiedad en la construccion del comunismo," *Marx Ahora: Revista Internacional* 16 (Havana, 2003).

25. Marx, *Grundrisse*, 287.

26. Karl Marx, *Economic and Philosophical Manuscripts of 1844,* in Marx and Engels, *Collected Works*, vol. 3 (New York: International Publishers, 1975), 302, 304.

27. Marx, *Grundrisse*, 488.

28. Ibid., 409.

29. Ibid., 711.

30. Ibid., 527, 708.

31. Ibid., 325.

32. Marx, *Capital*, vol. 1, 772.

33. Marx, *Grundrisse*, 488, 541, 708.

34. Karl Marx, *Critique of the Gotha Programme,* in Marx and Engels, *Selected Works*, vol. 2 (Moscow: Foreign Languages Publishing House, 1962), 24.

CHAPTER 2. THE PRODUCTION OF PEOPLE

1. Amartya Sen, *Inequality Reexamined* (Cambridge: Harvard University Press, 1992), 40.

2. Paolo Freire, *Pedagogy of the Oppressed* (New York: Continuum, 2006), 72.

3.   Ibid., 84, 86.

4.   Karl Marx, "Theses on Feuerbach," in Marx and Engels, *Collected Works*, vol. 6 (New York: International Publishers, 1976).

5.   Lucien Sève, *Man in Marxist Theory and the Psychology of Personality* (Sussex: Harvester Press, 1978), 304, 313.

6.   Marx, *Grundrisse*, 90-91, 287; Lebowitz, *Beyond CAPITAL*, 66-72.

7.   Marx, *Capital*, vol. 1, 772, 375.

8.   Marx, *Grundrisse*, 712.

9.   Lebowitz, *Beyond CAPITAL*, 178-81.

10. Ibid., 180-83.

11. Marx, *Grundrisse*, 494.

12. Marx, *Capital*, vol. 1, 283.

13. Marx, *Grundrisse*, 325.

14. Ibid., 410.

15. Marx, *Capital*, vol. 1, 447, 618.

16. Ibid., 739.

17. Marx, *Grundrisse*, 325, 409-10, 415-16.

18. Marx, *Capital*, vol. 3, 367.

19. Ibid., 178-79.

20. Marx, *Capital*, vol. 1, 450; Marx, *Grundrisse*, 453, 307.

21. Marx, *Grundrisse*, 694; Marx, *Capital*, vol. 1, 1053-54, 1058.

22. Marx, *Grundrisse*, 488.

23. Marx, *Capital*, vol. 1, 482-84, 548, 607-8, 614.

24. Ibid., 548, 643, 799.

25. Marx, *Grundrisse*, 488.

26. Marx, *Capital*, vol. 1, 899.

27. Lebowitz, *Beyond CAPITAL*, 181-84.

28. Marx, *Grundrisse*, 158.

29. Marx, *Capital*, vol. 1, 125.

30. Ibid., 772.

31. Ibid., 425.

32. Ibid., 617-18.

33. Marx, *Critique of the Gotha Programme*, 24.

34. Marx, *Capital*, vol. 1, 619.

35. Ibid., 643.

36. Ibid., 614.

37. Marx, *Critique of the Gotha Programme*, 24.

38. Mészáros, *Beyond Capital*, 817, 822.

39. Marx, *Capital*, vol. 1, 450, 173.

40. Marx, *Capital*, vol. 3, 178-79.

41. Marx, *Capital*, vol. 1, 173, 450, 482; Lebowitz, *Beyond CAPITAL*, 193-96.

42. Lebowitz, *Beyond CAPITAL*, 196.

43. Ibid., 201; see also chapter 7, "One-Sided Marxism," in *Beyond CAPITAL* for a discussion of one-sided concepts such as "unproductive labour."

44. Ibid., 200-202.

45. Lebowitz, *Build It Now*, 66.

46. Marx, *Capital*, vol. 1, 447.

47. Marx, "Inaugural Address of the Working Men's International Association," in Marx and Engels, *Collected Works*, vol. 20 (New York: International Publishers, 1985), 10-111; Lebowitz, , *Beyond CAPITAL*, chap. 5.

48. Marx, "Inaugural Address," 11; Marx, *Capital*, vol. 3, 511-12; Marx, *Theories of Surplus Value*, vol. 3 (Moscow: Progress Publishers, 1971), 497.

49. Marx, *Capital*, vol. 3, 571.

50. Marx, *Capital*, vol. I , 171.

51. This is, of course, a very brief and inadequate characterization. Extensive discussion of the Soviet Union and "Real Socialism" in general is part of the work in progress, "Studies in the Development of Socialism."

52. Jose. Broz Tito, "Factories to the Workers," *Socialist Thought and Practice* 15/6 (Belgrade, June 1975): 16.

CHAPTER 3. THE SOLIDARIAN SOCIETY

1. Adam Smith, *Wealth of Nations*, 14.

2. Karl Marx, "On the Jewish Question," in Marx and Engels, *Collected Works*, vol. 3 (New York: International Publishers, 1975), 162-64.

3. Karl Marx, "Comments on James Mill," in ibid., 217.

4. Ibid., 225-26.

5. Ibid., 225, 228.

6. Ibid., 227.

7. Marx, *Grundrisse*, 156-58.

8. Ibid., 158, 171-72.

9. Marx, *Capital*, vol. 3, 571; Lebowitz, *Beyond CAPITAL*, 88-89, 215.

10. Karl Marx, "Instructions to the Delegates of the Provisional General Council. The Different Questions," in *Minutes of the General Council of the First International, 1864-66* (Moscow: Foreign Languages Publishing House, n.d.), 346.

11. Karl Marx, *The Civil War in France,* in Marx and Engels, *On the Paris Commune* (Moscow: Progress Publishers, 1971), 76.

12. Marx, *Capital,* vol. 1, 171, emphasis added.

13. Ibid., 173.

14. Marx, *Critique of the Gotha Programme*, 23-4.
15. See the discussion in Michael A. Lebowitz, "Contradictions in the 'Lower Phase' of Communist Society," *Socialism in the World* 59 (Belgrade, 1987); and Michael A. Lebowitz, "La acumulacion originaria de relaciones comunistas," in *Marx Ahora: Revista Internacional* 11 (Havana, 2001).
16. Marx, *Critique of the Gotha Programme*, 23, 25.
17. Ibid., 23-24.
18. Marx, *Economic and Philosophic Manuscripts of 1844*, 241.
19. Marx and Engels, *The German Ideology*, 537-38.
20. Lebowitz, *Build It Now*, chap. 6.
21. Jose. Broz Tito, "Factories to the Workers," *Socialist Thought and Practice* 15/6 (Belgrade, June 1975): 4, 12-13.
22. Carlos Tablada, *Che Guevara: Economics and Politics in the Transition to Socialism* (Sydney, Aus.: Pathfinder, 1989), 111-12.
23. See a discussion of the general problem of differential access to the means of production in Michael A. Lebowitz, "El Pueblo y la propiedad en la construccion del comunismo," *Marx Ahora* 16 (Havana, 2003). The Yugoslavia experience is developed more fully in Lebowitz, *Studies in the Development of Socialism* (in progress).
24. Branko Horvat, *The Political Economy of Socialism* (Armonk, N.Y.: M. E. Sharpe, 1982), 238.
25. Tablada, *Che Guevara*, 92.
26. Marx, "On the Jewish Question," 154.
27. Ibid., 162-63.
28. "If you're happy, I'm happy" would be called a case of interdependent utility functions by neoclassical economists, but it plays very little role in their theoretical constructions. For example, if I get utility by seeing (and, indeed, making) you happy and disutility from seeing others unhappy (injured, starving), this comes under the category of aberrant and irrational behavior in a capitalist society—for example, "altruism" and "love"—and is accordingly marginalized.
29. Marx, "Comments on James Mill," 227-28.
30. Marx, *Economic and Philosophic Manuscripts of 1844,* 296, 298.
31. Ibid., 302.
32. Marx and Engels, *The German Ideology*, 255, 292.
33. Marx, *Grundrisse,* 172.
34. Ibid., 171-72.
35. Ibid., 158, 171.
36. Ibid., 172.
37. Ibid., 158-59.
38. Mészáros, *Beyond Capital*, 751.

39. Ibid., 758–59.
40. Lebowitz, *Build It Now*, 108.
41. Mészáros, *Beyond Capital*, 817.
42. Marx, *Grundrisse*, 158, 162.

CHAPTER 4. THE BEING AND BECOMING
OF AN ORGANIC SYSTEM

1. Marx, *Grundrisse*, 99–100; *The Poverty of Philosophy*, 167.
2. Lebowitz, *Beyond CAPITAL*, 52–4.
3. Marx, *Grundrisse*, 278.
4. Ibid.
5. Ibid., 459.
6. Ibid., 460.
7. Ibid., 460–61.
8. Ibid., 460.
9. Marx, *The Poverty of Philosophy*, 167.
10. It is well known that Hegel stated, "The truth is the whole." However, it is important to recognize that *he continued*: "The whole, however, is merely the essential nature reaching its completeness through the process of its own development." G.W.F. Hegel, *The Phenomenology of Mind* (New York: Harper Torchbooks, 1967), 75–76, 81.
11. Marx, *Grundrisse*, 278.
12. As noted earlier, Marx distinguished very clearly between the characteristics of capitalism and the process of "primitive accumulation" which "forms the pre-history of capital." Marx, *Capital*, vol. 1, 875.
13. Ibid., 899.
14. Marx, *Grundrisse*, 853, 859.
15. Marx, *Capital*, vol. 1, 900.
16. Ibid., 899, 935. As I have argued elsewhere, capital's ability to defeat the resistance of workers through spontaneous processes such as the market is not as absolute as Marx indicated; rather, capital must consciously divide and separate workers in order to reduce their ability to combine. See Michael A. Lebowitz, "The Politics of Assumption, the Assumption of Politics"; and Lebowitz, "Trapped Inside a Box? Five Questions for Ben Fine," *Historical Materialism* 18/1 (2010).
17. Marx, *Grundrisse*, 694, 699.
18. Marx, *Capital*, vol. 1, 382.
19. Ibid., 899.
20. Ibid., 911, 900.
21. Ibid., 935–96.
22. Karl Marx, *Economic Manuscript of 1861–63,* in Marx and Engels, *Collected Works*, vol. 30 (New York: International Publishers, 1988),

116; Lebowitz, *Beyond CAPITAL*, 124–30.

23. Marx, *Capital*, vol. 1, 716, 718.
24. Ibid., 771.
25. Ibid., 931.
26. Ibid., 927–28.
27. Ibid., 874, 1083.
28. Preobrazhensky's example of the problems inherent in such a combination was the interaction between the logic of commodity production and the logic of "primitive socialist accumulation"—tendencies which, in the case of growing agricultural production, generated a conflict between expansion of the consumer goods sector (Department II) and expansion of the sector producing means of production (i.e., Department I). Evgeny Preobrazhensky, *The New Economics* (Oxford: Clarendon Press, 1965), 176–77. Preobrazhensky's argument in the context of the becoming of vanguard relations of production is explored in Lebowitz, *Studies in the Development of Socialism*.
29. Marx, *Capital*, vol. 1, 899, 904, 905.
30. In "The Socialist Fetter Considered," presented to the Union of Radical Political Economists at ASSA in New Orleans, January 1992, I indicated that use of the terminology of the Regulation School was meant to indicate agreement with the importance they assign to social norms but not with their particular arguments. See also Alain Lipietz, *Mirages and Miracles: The Crises of Global Fordism* (London: Verso, 1987), 33; Alain Lipietz, "Reflections on a Tale: The Marxist Foundations of the Concepts of Regulation and Accumulation," *Studies in Political Economy* 26 (Summer 1988): 18–19.
31. Marx, *Capital*, vol. 1, 382, 899.
32. Ibid., 937. See also chap. 33 in vol. 1.
33. Ibid., 935–37. Note the discussion in Michael A. Lebowitz, "The Socialist Fetter: A Cautionary Tale," in *The Socialist Register 1991*, ed. Ralph Miliband and Leo Panitch (London: Merlin, 1991).
34. Marx, *Grundrisse*, 278.
35. Teodor Shanin, *Late Marx and the Russian Road: Marx and "The Peripheries of Capitalism"* (New York: Monthly Review Press, 1983), 49, 135–36.
36. Ibid., 62, 104–5.
37. Ibid., 101, 114, 117.

CHAPTER 5. THE CONCEPT OF A SOCIALIST TRANSITION

1. See http://www.departments.bucknell.edu/russian/const/36cons01.html.
2. V. I. Lenin, *The State and Revolution* (Peking: Foreign Languages Press, 1965), 112, 116.
3. Ibid., 114–15. Lenin did not limit himself to purely economic aspects, referring to what people become accustomed to, changes in the character of people and tradition; however, invariably the premise is the development of productive forces.
4. Marx, *Grundrisse*, 278. Emphasis added.
5. Marx, *Critique of the Gotha Programme*, 23–24.
6. See Michael A. Lebowitz, "Building on Defects: Theses on the Misinterpretation of Marx's Gotha Critique," *Science and Society* (October 2007). This discussion was presented originally at the 3rd International Conference on the Work of Karl Marx and the Challenges of the 21st Century in Havana, Cuba, 3–6 May 2006.
7. Note, for example, the earlier references to Michael A. Lebowitz, "La acumulacion originaria de relaciones comunistas" and "El Pueblo y la propiedad en la construccion del comunismo."
8. Marx, *Capital*, vol. 1, 171.
9. Lenin, *State and Revolution*, 95, 117.
10. Marx, *Economic and Philosophic Manuscripts of 1844*, 296–97, 306, 341–42; Marx to Ludwig Feuerbach, 11 August 1844, in Marx and Engels, *Collected Works* (1975), 354. For the record, on a personal level, I have no difficulty in describing myself as a communist, which represents for me an honorable tradition of the absolute commitment to build a socialist society—one that never loses sight of what capitalism is and how it destroys people.
11. See the discussion in chapter 11, "From Capital to the Collective Worker," in Lebowitz, *Beyond CAPITAL*.
12. Marx, "First Outline of *The Civil War in France*," 157.
13. Lebowitz, *Beyond CAPITAL,* chap. 5.
14. Ibid., 90–92, 96–98.
15. Marx and Engels, *The Communist Manifesto*, in Marx and Engels, *Collected Works*, Vol. 6. New York: International Publishers, 1976, 504.
16. In Michael A. Lebowitz, "Kornai and the Vanguard Mode of Production," *Cambridge Journal of Economics* 24/3 (May 2000), I introduced an alternative scenario in which a vanguard party that controls the state "seizes possession of production." In this case, rather than associated producers in possession of production, "vanguard relations of production" prevail and a "specifically vanguard mode of

production" emerges. My work in progress, *Studies in the Development of Socialism*, examines this phenomenon at length in its discussion of "Real Socialism."

17. Marx, "First Outline of *The Civil War in France*," 68–69; Lebowitz, *Beyond CAPITAL*, 193–96.

18. Lebowitz, *Beyond CAPITAL*, 189–96.

19. Marx, *The Civil War in France*, 75.

20. Karl Marx, "First Outline of *The Civil War in France*," in Marx and Engels, *On the Paris Commune*, 152–53.

21. Marx: *The Civil War in France*, 72–73; Lebowitz, *Beyond CAPITAL*, 193, 195.

22. Marx, *Critique of the Gotha Programme*, 32.

23. Marx, "First Outline of *The Civil War in France*," 152–54.

24. Marx, *Grundrisse*, 694, 699.

25. Marx, *Capital*, vol. 1, 799.

26. Ibid., 899.

27. Lebowitz, "The Socialist Fetter Considered"; and in *Studies in the Development of Socialism* (forthcoming).

28. Lebowitz, "The Socialist Fetter Considered." See chapter 7 of the present work for a more concrete discussion of a socialist mode of regulation.

29. Lebowitz, "The Socialist Fetter: A Cautionary Tale," 367; and in *Studies in the Development of Socialism* (forthcoming).

30. Tablada, *Che Guevara: Economics and Politics in the Transition to Socialism*, 92.

31. In one of the few explicit arguments offered, Branko Horvat proposed that ultimately the development of productive forces stimulated by distribution in accordance with contribution would lead to rising income and a diminishing marginal utility of income—thereby creating the basis for the principle of distribution in accordance with needs. The implicit assumption, of course, is that alienated needs to consume do not grow in accordance with alienated production. See Branko Horvat, *Towards a Theory of Planned Economy* (Beograd: Yugoslav Institute of Economic Research, 1964), 132–33.

32. Marx, *Critique of the Gotha Programme*, 23–24.

CHAPTER 6. MAKING A PATH TO SOCIALISM

1. Lenin, *The Right of Nations to Self-Determination*, in *Lenin: Selected Works*, vol. 1 (Moscow: Foreign Languages Publishing), 556.

2. Marx, *The Poverty of Philosophy*, 167.

3. Marx and Engels, *The German Ideology*, 53.

4. Lebowitz, *Beyond CAPITAL*, chap. 10.

5. I have described this as a "partial" charter because its starting point is capitalist relations of production, and it considers the alternative to these. Thus it does not address other inversions of human development such as patriarchy, caste society, and racism except implicitly.

6. Lebowitz, *Beyond CAPITAL*, 95–8, 89.

7. Lebowitz, *Build It Now*, 37–40.

8. Lebowitz, *Beyond CAPITAL*, 43.

9. Lebowitz, *Build It Now*, 66.

10. Opening the books to workers is also essential for effective taxation.

11. Michael A. Lebowitz, "The Capitalist Workday, the Socialist Workday," *MRZine*, April 2008.

12. Lebowitz, *Beyond CAPITAL*, 220.

13. Lebowitz, *Build It Now,* 39.

14. Marx and Engels, *The Communist Manifesto*, 504.

15. Lebowitz, *Beyond CAPITAL*, 192.

16. Oscar Lange, *On the Economic Theory of Socialism*, ed. Benjamin Lippincott (New York: McGraw-Hill, 1964), 123.

17. Marx and Engels, *The Communist Manifesto*, 504.

18. One can only laugh at those who think this is possible without taking the power of the state away from capital.

19. Recall Che's observation (noted in chapter 3) that each Yugoslav self-managed enterprise was "engaged in violent struggle with its competitors over prices and quality." When the goal is maximization of income per collective member, this is predictable.

20. A use-value is only a use-value when it is brought to the appropriate place, a place where it is needed.

21. Mészáros, *Beyond Capital*, 835.

22. Marx, *Critique of the Gotha Programme*, 23–24.

23. For example, see Elinor Ostrom, *Governing the Commons: The Evolution of Institutions for Collective Action* (Cambridge: Cambridge University Press, 1990); and Daniel W. Bromley, ed., *Making the Commons Work: Theory, Practice, Policy* (San Francisco: ICS Press, 1992).

24. Ostrom, *Governing the Commons*, 88.

CHAPTER 7. DEVELOPING A SOCIALIST MODE OF REGULATION

1. Iain Bruce poses this general question in his excellent book on Venezuela, *The Real Venezuela: Making Socialism in the 21st Century* (London: Pluto Press, 2008): "Is it possible to envisage the emergence of new state structures defending a new set of social interests, alongside or even within the old state which defends the old class interests?" (183).

2. István Mészáros, *The Challenge and Burden of Historical Time: Socialism in the Twenty-first Century* (New York: Monthly Review Press, 2008), 813–14.

3. Mészáros, *Beyond Capital*, 816–19.

4. Mészáros, *The Challenge and Burden of Historical Time*, 48, 55–59.

5. Ibid., 344.

6. Ibid., 59, 47.

7. Mészáros, *Beyond Capital*, 817.

8. Lebowitz, *Beyond CAPITAL*, 124–36. Emphasis upon reducing necessary labor in order to give us free time is a demand from within capitalism—one infected by capitalism because it is fixated upon the horror of the workday under capitalism. Contrary to Mészáros and others, the time for the full development of the individual should be understood not as "disposable time," "free time" that can be put to "creative use" by self-realizing individuals, but *directly social time*. In short, the focus should be not on the reduction of necessary labor but upon its *transformation*—a new, socialist definition of necessary labor, which incorporates "the time on a daily basis for education for self-managing, for our work within the household and our work within our communities" (Michael A. Lebowitz, "The Capitalist Workday, the Socialist Workday," *MRZine*, April 2008). With the abolition of capitalism, Marx acknowledged, necessary labor time "would expand to take up more of the day." Marx, *Capital*, vol. 1, 667.

9. The necessity of expedient actions at points is obvious. The costs of these (especially when extended beyond emergencies!) should be understood, and there should always be open recognition and discussion of those costs.

10. This discussion draws upon my presentation, "Building Upon Defects: Theses on the Misinterpretation of Marx's Gotha Critique," at the 3rd International Conference on the Work of Karl Marx and the Challenges of the 21st Century, in Havana, Cuba, 3–6 May 2006, and subsequently published in *Science & Society* (October 2007).

11. The discussion in this section comes directly from "Organisational Implications," a section (177–80) of "The Politics of *Beyond CAPITAL*," in Michael A. Lebowitz, *Historical Materialism* 14/4 (2006). This response to the symposium on *Beyond CAPITAL* in *Historical Materialism* 14/2 (2006) was reproduced in the Afterword to the Turkish edition of the book.

12. Lebowitz, "The Politics of *Beyond CAPITAL*," 177–78.

13. Lebowitz, *Build It Now*, chapter 7, "The Revolution of Radical Needs: Behind the Bolivarian Choice of a Socialist Path." See Marta Harnecker's discussion of "a body to coordinate all the different

emancipatory social practices," in Harnecker, *Rebuilding the Left* (London: Zed Books, 2007), chap. 10, "Characteristics of the New Political Instrument."

14. See the discussion of the practice of Leninist parties in Latin America in Harnecker, *Rebuilding the Left*.

15. Ibid., 88.

16. Lebowitz, "Socialism Doesn"t Drop from the Sky," *Build It Now: Socialism for the 21st Century*, chap. 5.

17. See the discussion of vanguard relations of production in Lebowitz, "Kornai and the Vanguard Mode of Production"; and in Lebowitz, *Studies in the Development of Socialism* (forthcoming).

18. Lebowitz, *Beyond CAPITAL*, 179–84.

Index